PLAYTHINGS AS LEARNING TOOLS

A Parents' Guide

Joan P. Isenberg
and
Judith E. Jacobs
George Mason University

Wiley Parent Education Series
Mark Spikell, Editor

1807 1982

John Wiley & Sons, Inc.
New York • Chicester • Brisbane • Toronto • Singapore

Library of Congress Cataloging in Publication Data:

Isenberg, Joan P., 1941-
    Playthings as learning tools.

    Wiley Parent Education Series

    1. Play.   2. Child Development.
3. Educational games.   4. Educational toys.
I. Jacobs, Judith E., 1943-
II. Title.
HQ782. I79   155.4′18   81-13121
ISBN 0-471-09042-5   AACR2

Printed in the United States of America

    82 83   10   9   8   7   6   5   4   3   2   1

This book was written
for
all of the children
and
the children in all of us
with
special thoughts
for
Jennifer and Michelle

Copyright Notices and Acknowledgments

Foreword

It is no secret that the twenty-year period from 1960 to 1980 has resulted in a crisis of confidence in the American educational system at all levels. Criticism of the formal schooling process comes from the media, politicians, the public at large, and even educators. While specific charges vary from one locality to another, the general message is the same: students are not adequately prepared to function in today's complex world. Critics charge that students cannot read, write, or compute; that they are unable to reason, think, make decisions, or solve problems. In short, the critics claim, today's students lack the basic skills necessary to live and work as productive, contributing members of our democratic society.

Whether completely true or not, the criticism of our educational system is perceived by the majority of the public as being accurate. Does the public's perception mean the American educational system is doomed to failure? Hardly! Rather, it suggests that all concerned citizens must join together to help improve the system and enhance educational opportunities for our nation's youth. It suggests, further, that we cannot rely upon schools alone for the education of our children. We, as parents and concerned citizens, can and must participate actively in the education of our youth. To that end, the forward looking editors at John Wiley & Sons, Inc. have made an exciting, bold commitment to improving education by creating the Wiley Parent Education Series.

The Wiley Parent Education Series is a collection of specially prepared books for parents written by outstanding educators. These books are unique because they deal with important educational topics for parents who are interested in supplementing their children's formal schooling experiences. Books already in the series focus upon the topics of playthings, television, reading, and microcomputers; other topics being considered include career development, critical thinking skills, and problem solving. The books are not primarily "how to" or recipe books telling parents exactly what to do for some educational objective. Instead, each book in the series is intended to provide important, up-to-date information for adults—parents and teachers—who want to help children grow and develop intellectually. The books present thoughtful, educationally sound ideas about what youngsters need. Numerous specific activities are included which can be used to engage children in fruitful, educational explorations that supplement but do not replace what may happen at school.

It is perhaps fitting and proper that the first book in the Parent Education Series is *Playthings As Learning Tools*. As authors Isenberg and Jacobs aptly note, play is a major vehicle by which children learn. Since play and education begin before children enter school and both continue through adulthood, initiating the Series by exploring the learning potential of play and playthings lays the foundation for a productive, long-term educational relationship between parent and child.

Mark A. Spikell
Series Editor

Table of Contents

Appendices

Preface

All children play; and play, at any age, is natural and should be fun. Play is also the major vehicle through which young children learn. When your children tell you that they "just played" in school, do you often wonder what they learned?

The purpose of this book is to help you understand what children can learn from play. We strongly believe that play teaches more than how to "just play." Play is more than just "having fun." It is this belief that motivated the writing of this book.

Play can occur at any time or in any place; it bears directly on the development of such fundamentals as the learning of language and mathematical ideas and the development of thinking skills and social roles. This book focuses on how playthings and play activities contribute to children's intellectual development. We want to state at the outset, however, that play also contributes to children's physical, social, and emotional development. We recognize that play is important to all these areas. But here we consider the contribution of play to one area of development, that is, intellectual growth, or what children can learn.

Children play not only with commercial toys and games but also with things most adults would not consider toys or games. Any adult can go to a toy department and select an educational toy or game for children of a certain age level. Not all adults, however, understand how playing with that toy can contribute to children's intellectual development. It is even more likely that most adults do not understand how playing with common everyday objects can be more educational than playing with the most expensive educational toy.

Since children are taught by both parents and teachers, there is a need for both groups to pay attention to the learning potential of play and playthings.

- Parents need to understand why play is important for their children's intellectual development.
- Parents need to understand why playtime is an important part of the school day.

11

This book will help parents:
- Identify the kinds of learning that can occur through children's play.
- Create environments that encourage children to play.
- Guide children's play in order to make the most of the opportunities for learning.

The activities presented in this book are child-centered rather than adult-centered. We believe that the most appropriate role that parents can play in promoting children's development is a non-directive, supportive one. By *non-directive*, we mean that parents ask questions and make suggestions rather than give specific instructions, and that the child, not the adult, selects the play activities. By *supportive*, we mean that the parents provide the tools, environment, and encouragement that permit children to learn through play.

Most of the activities in this book are natural and spontaneous ones; many of them use materials not typically thought of as playthings. This emphasis is in contrast to the highly commercialized and increasingly technological world in which today's children live. The authors' choice of such activities results from our belief that children can learn from their play no matter how ordinary and simple their activities seem to adults.

The completion of this book would not have been possible without the support and help of many people. Though it is impossible to thank each of them here, there are those whose contributions deserve special recognition.

We are especially grateful to those who read the preliminary drafts and provided invaluable comments. The efforts of Esther Jacobs, Barbara and Leon Leake, Barbara Silver Levy, and Carol Skillman are warmly acknowledged.

We also owe a debt of gratitude to the staff and children of Mount Daniel Elementary School, Falls Church, Virginia, and Prince of Peace Lutheran Day School, Springfield, Virginia, for their cooperation. Special thanks are given to Marianne Latall, director of Prince of Peace, and to William Thomas, principal of Mount Daniel.

The writing of Chapter 6, Commercial Toys and Games, was greatly facilitated by the assistance of Douglas Thomson, President of the Toy Manufacturers of America, Inc., and those manufacturers who provided us with both information and material for review. We thank them for their help.

There would have been no book without the encouragement, support, and efforts of the Series Editor, Mark Spikell. We are greatly appreciative of all he did at each crucial stage in the development of the text.

To George Mason University and its support staff and facilities provided for the writing efforts of its faculty, we are grateful.

One final note: many recent books mention that they are using the pronoun "he" in the generic sense, meaning both he and she, boys and girls, men and women. We have very carefully chosen not to use either he or she in this book. Play is important for all children's development and if, as we believe, they are to grow up free from stereotypes, then we, as adults, must make every effort to create a world without limits. By writing this book in a non-sexist way, we hope to have expanded the number of options all children will have in their play.

J.P.I.
J.E.J.

Part I Learning Begins with Play

Chapter 1   An Introduction to Play and Playthings

How Parents Can Help Their Children Play

PLAY IS AN IMPORTANT PART of every child's life. Young children spend many hours involved in some kind of play. Parents, as children's first playmates, have an important role in helping their children benefit from play. Here are several ways you can enrich your children's play experiences. The following suggestions, taken as a group, can make your children's playtimes more productive.

Watch Your Children Play. This is the best way to get to know your own children. You can learn who their favorite playmates are, what their favorite playthings are, what themes they like to act out, and what seems to trouble them in their play. Knowing these things can help you create a play environment especially suited to your children and of greatest benefit to them.

Be a Model for Playfulness. Since parents are children's first playmates, children learn first from them. Their play comes mainly through imitating adults. You can stimulate your children's play by being a model for playfulness. If children need help playing at grocery store shopping, show them how you would pretend to be some of the various people in a grocery store. Ask questions or make suggestions in order to keep their play going.

Play with Your Children. Playing with your children tells you many things. Because you have been part of their play, you can learn about their likes and dislikes and be more able to select toys or suggest materials appropriate to their level of play. Remember that the play must be kept at the child's level. If it goes to your level, it could hinder rather than enhance children's play.

Expand the Scope of Your Children's Play. When you are part of your children's play, you know their interests and skills. You may want to suggest some new ideas or give them something different to play with. Then let them decide if and when they want to take your suggestions. Sometimes they reject adult ideas, and you should respect that. Such a refusal shows that children are making decisions and choices on their own. When offering ideas to expand the scope of your children's play, you would do better to suggest possibilities rather than specifics. Rather than saying, "Would you like to give this sick baby some medicine?", which will probably get a negative response, you might comment, "Here is a sick baby who really needs some medicine." Let the child decide what to do with that situation. As a parent, you have a better chance of moving children's play along if you approach the play situation with suggestions rather than directions.

Support Children in Their Play. Let your children know that you value their play and playthings. There are many ways to do this. Encourage and praise them when they use playthings constructively. Show interest in what they are doing. If children want to play alone, let them. If they ask for help, take the time to give that help. Be willing to leave the play situation alone once children no longer need your help.

Plan for Your Children's Play. Planning for play greatly enhances it. Here are some of the ways you can plan for your children's play:

- Give children a place to keep their playthings. A low shelf can be helpful, because it allows children to take down and put away playthings by themselves.
- Help children keep their playthings organized. Clutter does not encourage play.
- Use old shoe boxes to hold small toys and to keep things organized and accessible.
- Provide opportunities for children to play with other children. Children learn from each other. They need many opportunities to be with other children.
- Provide a variety of play experiences. Children need time both for playing alone and with others. They also need a balance of active and quiet play activities.
- Provide a balance of child-selected and adult-selected play activities. Children should have many

chances to choose what they will do for their play. Though they can benefit from adult-selected play, they are learning independence and self-reliance when they have the responsibility for making decisions about how they spend their time.

Encourage Your Children to Make-believe. Most children like to pretend. They play mommy, daddy, doctor, astronaut. For most children, this pretend play is natural and spontaneous. Parents can encourage children's pretend play. By supplying children with a box of unwanted clothes and some other props for dress-ups, you are helping children to pretend. More importantly, though, you are telling children that you approve of such play. For those children who do not freely engage in make-believe play, you can encourage them by sharing some of the pretend games you played when you were a child.

Encourage Your Children to Talk about Their Play. Language helps children in many ways. It helps them imitate adult speech; it enhances pretend play; it helps children control the direction of their play; and it adds new words to their vocabulary.

One of the most important ways you can help your children is to talk with them. Children need the stimulation of adult language and ideas. Talk about the colors in their clothes, the books they are reading, or their trip to the doctor. All experiences can be shared.

When children ask questions, take the time to answer them completely, yet briefly. Give them a chance to participate in the conversation. Check to see if you have answered their question before going into greater detail. Too much explanation can lead them to expect that all the answers come from adults. This stifles independence. Children need experience in finding their own answers to some of their questions.

Mealtime and bedtime are particularly good times to have extended conversations. Encourage them to talk about things in detail. You might say, "Tell me more about the game you were playing with your friends. It looked like fun when you were chasing the balls."

These suggestions can help you play an active role in increasing the benefits your children gain from their play experiences. In the following sections, there are specific suggestions about how you can use this book to help you help your children learn through their play.

How to Use This Book

ORGANIZATION OF THE BOOK

This book is organized into three parts. Part I is a general introduction to play and playthings.

Part II describes in detail the play activities that young children enjoy. These descriptions have been divided into a chapter on indoor activities and one on outdoor activities.

Part III describes the games and toys that young children play with. These have been grouped into three chapters: on card games, rhyming and chanting games, and commercial games and toys.

Each chapter describes the playthings and play activities and how and what these activities can contribute to children's learning.

Appendix A contains a chart that lists specific skills, such as classifying, and indicates which activities in Chapters 2 through 6 help to develop that skill. This could assist you in selecting appropriate activities for helping children to learn specific skills and concepts. Also included in Appendix A is a glossary of terms used in the sections of this book called *possible learning outcomes*. Appendix B provides a list of common household objects and junk materials that can be used as playthings. Again, the materials listed are cross-referenced to specific activities described in the book so that you will know what can be done with those empty egg cartons. Appendix C lists manufacturers of children's playthings with a brief notation of particular products appropriate for young children. Appendix D lists other resources that may be of interest to readers of this book.

WAYS OF APPROACHING THE BOOK

You can read this book from cover to cover and increase your understanding of young children, how they develop, and how play helps them learn. The detailed descriptions of specific play activities can further increase your understanding.

Another approach to this book is to explore one kind of play or one type of plaything at a time. If your children enjoy playing in the kitchen and you want to know what they are learning from those pots and pans as the noise gets louder, then you might turn directly to activity 2.9. There you can discover not only what they are learning, but also how to further that learning by introducing some additional playthings or asking them questions. On the other hand, if your children are fascinated by playing cards but seem not to be following any rules in their card games, you might turn to Chapter 4, which discusses why card games appeal to children and describes numerous card games for young children to play.

A third approach to this book is to concentrate on a specific skill or concept that you want your children to work on. By using Appendix A, you can identify the particular skill in the left-hand column of the chart and then find the activities and playthings that can foster that skill or help to develop that concept. If you are concerned with developing classification skills, you will find specific activities listed in each of the chapters. If you have a collection of buttons or empty containers and want to know how to use them, turn to Appendix B to find where in this book there are descriptions of specific activities which use these materials.

ABOUT THE ACTIVITIES

Chapters 2 through 6 contain many detailed descriptions of children's play activities. Each activity is independent of every other activity. They are only examples of some of the kinds of play children do. Whether your children enjoy a particular activity depends upon their interests and abilities. Not all children will enjoy all the activities.

Children will, however, repeat, over and over again, each activity that they do enjoy. This repetition is important. It enables children to practice new skills until they become comfortable doing them. It makes them feel confident when they can do something easily. They will want to share their successes with you. It is desirable to let them repeat activities at which they are successful, rather than rushing them on to new activities.

The activities included in this book are appropriate for both girls and boys. All children need experiences with as many different playthings as possible. Boys can gain many skills through sewing activities; girls learn many things from building with blocks. Both girls and boys enjoy and benefit from acting out different roles. Whether they choose to be doctors or police officers, fire fighters or teachers, acting out these parts helps them learn. In letting children select their play activities from the whole range of possibilities, you can help them explore more of the options that are available to them.

The descriptions of activities contain many possibilities for children's play, but children are wonders, and you can never anticipate everything they can think of. The descriptions only suggest what *may* happen as children play, not what definitely will happen.

As you read through the activities in Chapters 2 and 3, you will notice that the descriptions of most activities are divided into levels. The levels describe a child's typical progression through that one particular activity. Level 1 in the button-sorting activity is unique to button sorting and children who are at Level 1 in button sorting may be at Level 2 in block play. Therefore, these levels are not general developmental levels. They are specific to a given activity and are not necessarily related to the child's age.

Following the description of each activity is a list of *possible learning outcomes*. These outcomes are the most important things that children may learn through the repetition of the activities. Not all possibilities are listed. The ones given only suggest the kinds of learning that can occur.

Many of the *possible learning outcomes* include the special vocabulary often used by teachers. A general discussion of many of these terms appears at the end of this chapter. A glossary of these special terms is included in Appendix A, where each term is followed by an explanation of its meaning and an example that illustrates it. Familiarity with this special vocabulary can help parents better understand what teachers mean when they describe their pupils' learning.

These learning outcomes are not taught directly. They are an outgrowth of the play experience and provide a foundation upon which children build later, more formal learning. It is not advisable to try to teach these outcomes or to test whether children have learned the skills involved.

The following sections present the theoretical basis of this book in a discussion of play and playthings and their impact on children's thinking.

What Are Play and Playthings?

Play is children's work. It is a natural and important activity for them. Play is how they learn about their world. Through many repeated play experiences, children can clarify and master many fundamental physical, social, and intellectual skills and concepts.

For any activity to be considered play, it must be enjoyable, voluntary, and active. This applies to all play, whether children's or adults'. When children play, they must first of all enjoy what they are doing or their activity is not play. Second, when they play, children must participate freely and willingly in the play activity. Third, play is a form of behavior — something one does, an activity one is involved in. When they áre actively involved in their play and decide for themselves what and how they will play, children have one of their few opportunities to control their own experiences.

Play is an end in itself. Children at play are concerned primarily with what they are doing and how they are doing it; they are not usually interested in the result of their play. The value of play lies in the process of doing it. But while playing, children learn more than just how to play, and they learn more than facts; they learn how to learn. While playing, they are learning many specific ideas and skills in incidental ways. This book focuses on the incidental learning that children gain as they play.

In this book, a plaything is defined in its broadest sense: it is anything a child plays with. It can be water, a measuring cup, or a store-bought toy. Playthings are simply those things, found or bought, that help children play.

Some adults assume that children should play only with commercial toys and do not encourage children to play with common, everyday objects. A valuable plaything is one that stimulates and interests children, is somewhat different from other playthings, and can be used in more than one way. Such a plaything is called "open-ended" in the sense that it is not restricted to just one use. As long as an object meets these criteria for a valuable plaything, parents can be assured that it will enhance their children's play and learning. Therefore, it is not necessary to spend large sums of money on commercial toys for children. Playthings are found everywhere. Children enjoy using discarded materials as playthings as much as they enjoy a store-bought toy.

Through play and playthings, the learning process begins. Playthings by themselves do not teach. It is the process of playing that helps children learn; playthings are the tools that help this process. Through children's interactions with playthings and people, they develop specific skills, concepts, and ideas. Playthings give children the chance to use some basic skills. For example, they provide many opportunities for making decisions, such as what to play with, how to play with it, and whether to play alone or with a friend. All the while, playthings help children have fun while learning and solving problems.

Playthings have an important effect on the course of children's play. Whatever the toy or plaything (see Guidelines for Selecting and Using Playthings in Chapter 6), it can either encourage children's play or deter it. "Open-ended" playthings, which can be used in more than one way—dress-ups, collage materials, water, or sand—help children play, but toys with limited possibilities—a wind-up toy or a make-up kit—can actually inhibit or limit children's play.

In order for play and playthings to encourage children's intellectual growth, they must enable children to do things for themselves and to make choices. Children of different ages can use the same basic play materials. Most homes, yards, and neighborhoods have many things that interest children that they can play with and learn from. Play is important for all children. It is their major source of learning in the preschool and primary grade years. The use of many different kinds of playthings helps children gain the greatest benefit from their play.

How Playthings Help Children Think

Children's thinking differs from adult thinking. Children are making the transition to the more formal processes of reasoning, making inferences, and problem solving that are characteristic of adult thought. Children's thinking, though, has definite characteristics. Children whose mental development has reached the same point think about and react to situations in very similar ways. Young children begin to use symbols and spend much time in fantasy play. Language use increases dramatically and their communication with other children and with adults comes more easily. For example, as children interact with a ball by pushing it back and forth, they learn how to control the ball as well as being able to think ahead and plan what they want to do while playing ball. As children interact with people by talking and playing with them, they learn to think about what they are going to say or how they are going to play with them.

There is, though, no such thing as a typical four-year-old. Some children develop more quickly than others. A child who is socially advanced may be physically or intellectually less developed than another child of the same age. Despite young children's rapid increase in language and communication skills, their thinking and reasoning processes have a number of limitations. How these limitations affect their thinking depends on their level of development and not necessarily on their age.

One limitation of children's thought is that it is *perceptually based*. This means that they think about things only in terms of what they actually see. For them, a bigger box is assumed to be heavier than a smaller box and a sandwich cut into two parts is thought to be more than the whole sandwich.

Another limitation is that their thought is *egocentric*. Children believe that everybody sees the world and thinks about it the same way they do. As a result, children have difficulty seeing others' points of view. Their self-centered behavior comes from their being absorbed in themselves. Thus, when children describe something that has happened to them, they often leave out many details; they assume the other person knows everything that they know. When they repeat what is said by the people around them, they often do this not to communicate with others but for the enjoyment of thinking out loud while playing.

Through repeated social interactions, children become less egocentric. Disagreements often push them into seeing another person's point of view. Fantasy play also helps them develop other ways of seeing things and brings them to a higher level of thinking. Young children increase their independence through their explorations of the world. As they develop, they eventually give up some of their egocentric thinking.

Young children's thinking is further limited by *centering*, a way of thinking that involves focusing on only one characteristic of an object or event. What adults think of as "wrong" answers to questions or cute comments are simply products of young children's way of thinking. For example, they assume that a taller glass always holds more soda than does a shorter, wider glass because they are focusing on how high the level of soda is in the glass. They believe that an adult standing behind them is hidden from everyone's view because they are standing in front of the adult. Young children ignore the fact that the adult's greater height makes the adult visible.

Children's thinking is enhanced by learning and acquiring knowledge. Such knowledge is gained through children's interactions with the people and things in their world. Play is the major way that children acquire knowledge. Research shows that children who are deprived of play experiences do not learn as effectively as children who do know how to play.

Play and playthings are as important to the development of children's thinking as food and fresh air are to their physical development. Children use play and playthings to acquire new information and make it a part of themselves. As children play with other children and with playthings, they see how the world works in new and different ways and they begin to form fundamental concepts. For example, as children play in the bathtub with various sizes of plastic containers, they can develop an understanding of the concepts of volume and quantity.

Play and playthings also offer children many opportunities for making decisions. In a world that requires more and more decision making and selection from among choices, children who have many opportunities to play will have many opportunities to practice decision making.

One of the important ways that children learn is by watching others. Much of children's playtime is spent imitating people. Playing house, dressing-up in their parents' clothes, and mimicking adults at work and play are typical of such play. Each of these activities allows children to learn how people and things behave.

Such modeling or imitating behavior permits children to learn new behaviors as well as to practice old, existing ones. This type of play enables children to learn from other people by interacting with them. Such experiences improve children's ability to get along with people, thereby increasing the resources available to them.

As children repeat activities and respond to them in different ways, they develop an exploratory, "let's find out" attitude. As children play, their play becomes more complex. This longer, more involved play is accompanied by an increase in their ability to concentrate and to stay with a task until it is completed.

Besides the general ways in which play helps children learn to think, there are more specific ways in which they learn from play. Some of this learning occurs in the areas of language and vocabulary development, number and measurement ideas, thinking skills, symbolic thought, and perceptual-motor skills.

Language and Vocabulary Development

Language and vocabulary development are necessary for good communication. The ability to communicate is important to all aspects of learning. Communication means both talking with others and understanding what others are saying. To be able to do both of these things, children need to know the meanings of words and ideas.

As children have more opportunities and experiences, they begin to form their own ideas about things. These ideas become associated with specific words. Through words, people exchange or express ideas, needs, or wishes. As they learn new words and clarify ideas, children gain a better understanding of their world.

Speech, or oral language, is the way young children share their ideas. The more opportunities children have to listen to others, the more they are able to develop their communication skills. When children play alone, they talk to themselves about what they are doing because it is important to them. When playing with an adult or other children, they have many opportunities to listen and take in information from someone else's point of view. Play helps children develop the language skills that help them get along with others. In turn, this enhances the value of their play.

As their communication skills develop, they begin to realize that symbols can be used to represent real objects and that a spoken word stands for something. Children often use a toy car when talking about their family's real car. The toy represents for them the actual car. Children learn what is meant by a word, such as "fork" and are able to select this object when it is mentioned. The use of symbols is critical for learning how to read. The ability to hold mental images from one's past experiences in one's head and to recall them when a word is spoken makes it easier to associate that mental image or idea with the printed word. This is why developing communication skills is essential to learning how to read.

NUMBER AND MEASUREMENT IDEAS

Number and measurement ideas enable people to order the world in a quantitative way. As part of their language and vocabulary development, children learn the ideas and words that describe the world in quantitative terms. Children talk about who has more or who is first or last. In addition, their play experiences allow them to learn some mathematical ideas. They learn how to answer the question "How many?" by counting objects such as blocks or buttons. In this way, they learn about numbers. Children learn about measurement when they determine the length of an object by counting the number of blocks in a tower or the number of cups of water it takes to fill a jar. All this learning is incidental to their play but is an important by-product of it.

THINKING SKILLS

One of the major benefits of play is its impact on the development of thinking skills. When children play, they ask many questions about what they are doing and what they are using. What is important is not the conclusions that they reach, which may be right or wrong, but the thinking involved in reaching those conclusions. The more children explore their environment, the more they think of questions and the more they search for answers. Many of these questions and their answers are never put into words. Play and playthings help children find their own answers to many of their questions.

One way children show this reasoning ability is through classification, the process of organizing the world into categories.

This ability develops gradually as children begin to put things together according to similarities or differences or to arrange groups of objects according to characteristics such as color, size, or shape. The development of classification is important to children's thinking because it is the basis of all thinking and reasoning processes and is an integral part of the development of mathematical concepts.

SYMBOLIC THOUGHT

Children need to be able to create mental images of the things and people in their world. These images are used to represent real objects. Such images are necessary to the development of their thinking and are essential to learning how to read and use numbers. Symbolic thought is the process of mentally recalling an object that is no longer visible. As children develop the ability to think symbolically, that is, to create mental images, their thinking is no longer tied only to what they see. This enables them to use past experiences in their present world.

It is easier to remember what a word means if one has a picture in one's mind of what that word represents. Holding an image in one's mind is also essential for meaningful communication. Language requires children to picture reality in their minds. The word *doll* is a symbol for the actual plaything and brings to mind a mental picture of it. The word *three* and the symbol 3 should bring to mind a mental picture of that number of objects. Both reading and mathematics involve associating an idea in a mental picture with a word. Pretend play is the major vehicle for developing symbolic thought in young children.

Another by-product of pretend play is the development of flexibility in one's thinking. Children's responses must change when there are changes in the rules of their play or the situations in which they imagine themselves. Flexibility and adaptability are skills that all people need. Play gives children a chance to try out these skills.

PERCEPTUAL-MOTOR SKILLS

Children learn by taking in information through their senses. As they play, they look, smell, touch, taste, and listen to their playthings. They acquire information from their environment through their senses. This information is used by the brain to tell the body's muscles what to do. This coordinated activity is called perceptual-motor development. Such skills as eye-hand coordination, visual discrimination, and visual memory are important for young children's learning.

Play activities can help children develop their perceptual-motor skills. For example, button-sorting activities help develop eye-hand coordination and visual skills that are needed for fast and fluent reading. Pretending to make lunch for a friend helps develop visual memory skills that are important for vocabulary development, communication, understanding the printed word, and the development of number ideas.

Play is a child's work. First and foremost, it should be fun. But play is more than just fun. Play is the way children learn about themselves and the world in which they live. As children play, they are learning how to learn as well as developing greater self-awareness and thinking and communication skills. Play, playthings, and learning are so intertwined they cannot be separated. Play and playthings are children's tools for learning to live in this world. Use this book to gain a better understanding of your children's world as they gain a better understanding of the world of grown-ups.

Part II   Play Activities

Introduction to Part II

CHAPTERS 2 AND 3 DESCRIBE some typical indoor and outdoor activities of young children. The activities in each chapter are listed alphabetically; each of them is independent of the others. All children, both girls and boys, can benefit from each of these activities. Most likely, your children will, at one time or another, do most of them.

All these activities are presented in the same format. Following the name of the activity and a listing of the necessary materials, there is a detailed description of a typical progression through that activity. This progression is divided into levels and indicates how children often develop in their use of the materials. The levels of one activity are in no way related to the levels of any other activity. Different children will spend varying amounts of time on any given level. This is because children's interests and abilities vary. The more experience children have with a particular activity, the more likely it is that they will move on to the next level. Therefore, none of these levels can be matched to specific ages.

Following the description of the activity is a listing of *possible learning outcomes* that children can reach after repeated experiences with that activity. Although many specific learning outcomes are identified, they do not represent every possibility. This list suggests what can occur and it can help you appreciate how your children's play contributes to their cognitive development. Not all children will learn thoroughly each outcome listed. Some will learn many of them, others will only begin to become familiar with the ideas. Therefore, it is important that children enjoy their play without being asked to show what they have learned.

At the end of each activity there is a list of some alternate materials that children can use to have similar play experiences from which the same kinds of learning outcomes can occur. Again, the materials listed are the most commonly available ones and do not include all possible alternate materials that could be used.

Children are challenged by activities that may appear simple to adults. They also enjoy repeating these activities over and over again. It is important for them to have the freedom to choose how they spend their time, because much of what they choose is precisely what benefits them the most.

Chapter 2   Indoor Activities

2.1   Button Sorting

MATERIALS

An assortment of 30 buttons, some duplicates
An egg carton

DESCRIPTION

Children enjoy playing with buttons. A collection of many different kinds of buttons lets children explore and discover many things. Their play with buttons will be useful in their later learning.

Level 1

At first, children will simply play with the buttons. They may spread them out, covering as much space as possible; they may make piles of buttons according to some rules they have made up; or they may try to stack buttons, one on top of another. No matter what they do with the buttons, from this free play they are learning the many different properties of buttons.

The egg carton may be used as a place to keep the buttons. Its sections may be used to organize the buttons in several different ways. A closed egg carton may be used to mix up the buttons so that when they are dumped out they look like a new set of buttons.

Level 2

After playing with the buttons and grouping them by different rules, children can be helped to consolidate their learning. You can use their play with buttons to help them learn some new words.

You might have the following discussions with your children: "This is a *white* button. Show me some other *white* buttons. Show me a button that is *not white.*" (Then you can name the color of the button shown.) "Here is a *big* button. Show me a button that is *not big.* We call this button *small.*"

You can encourage your children to explain themselves and improve their communication skills by asking them why they did certain things. For example, if children pile up some buttons but not others, ask, "Why did you put these buttons together?"

You can pick out a button, such as one with two holes, and ask children to put all the other buttons with two holes in the egg carton. Keep available the one you selected so that the children can see and be reminded of what they are to find.

You can change this activity by using buttons of various colors, shapes, textures (rough, smooth), materials (fabric, plastic, wood), and sizes.

Level 3

Children need to repeat all the activities listed in Level 2 so they can master those skills and concepts. One idea they have difficulty with is *seriation*, the process of putting objects in size order. The following activity could be used to help them with this skill. This work should go very slowly.

Pick out three buttons as different in size as possible. Put the others out of sight. Ask for the biggest button. Then ask for the smallest. Place these far apart on the work area. Ask where the third button goes. Then place the third button between the other two.

Where does the C button go?

With older children, five to seven years, you can ask them which of the buttons is the biggest, which is the next biggest, and which is the smallest. Or you can ask that the buttons be placed in size order, biggest to smallest.

You can also do these activities by having the buttons arranged from smallest to biggest. Add a fourth, fifth, and then sixth button after children can do the three-button activities easily.

Level 4

If you want to help your children get ready for counting and understanding numbers, you can do many activities with them. While these activities are not really play activities, they do use the materials with which children play.

1. When using the egg carton for storing buttons, you may notice that children want to put *at least* one button in each section. This kind of activity is often followed by placing one, and *only one*, button in each of the twelve compartments, leaving the other, unused buttons on the side. You could develop this with specific suggestions:

"Place *some* buttons in each section of the egg carton."
(You do not care whether all the buttons are used or how many are placed in each compartment.)

"Place only *one* button in each section of the egg carton."

2. Use a piece of index card, about 1 inch by 3 inches. Draw a picture of one button and write the numeral "1" under it. On

Learning numbers
using buttons

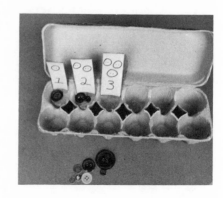

another piece of an index card, draw a picture of two buttons and write the numeral "2" under it. Do the same for up to six buttons. Place the cards showing one, two, and three buttons in a row, right next to each other.

Show the children how you can match one real button with the picture of one button while you say how many buttons are in that section: "one button." Do the same for two buttons, saying how many buttons are in that section: "two buttons." Do the same for three buttons.

Empty the buttons from the egg carton and, with the cards in place, ask the child to do what you just did, to match the picture with the right number of buttons.

When that can be done easily, try the activity without the cards. Say, "Put one button in this section," Put two buttons in the next section," and so on. Then try this with four buttons, then five buttons and even more. With practice, older children will be able to do this for all twelve sections.

As you talk about these activities, mention that each compartment has one more button than the compartment before: "Two buttons is one more button than one button," "Three buttons is more button than two buttons."

Possible Learning Outcomes

Ideas and Their Vocabulary
Names of colors: red, green
Names of textures: rough, smooth
Quantitative and comparative words: large, small, medium, number names (two)
Names of materials: metal, plastic, wood

Number Ideas
One-to-one correspondence: placing one button in each section
One more than: placing one button in the first section, two in the next, and so forth

Counting: number of holes in buttons, number of buttons
  in a pile
Cardinality: "fourness", knowing that there are four buttons, no matter what size or shape they are

Thinking Skills
  Classifying: putting buttons together by color, size,
    shape, texture, or number of holes
  Seriation: putting buttons in order by size, largest to
    smallest or smallest to largest

ALTERNATE MATERIALS
  Coins: U.S. or foreign, pennies, nickels, dimes
  Colored paper scraps
  Uncooked macaroni and noodles
  Beans: lima, pinto, kidney
  Fabric scraps
  M & M candies

2.2 Collage

MATERIALS
  Sheets of paper
  Glue or paste
  Scissors
  Scraps of paper, cloth, and other material
  Popsicle sticks
  Buttons
  Toilet paper rolls

DESCRIPTION
  A collage is a collection of materials pasted on a sheet of
paper or cardboard. The materials are placed on the surface in
such a way as to make a design.
  Children enjoy making collages because no matter how they
do it they are right; there is no set way of doing things. They cut
and tear and then paste many different kinds of materials onto a
surface. They make the materials do what they want them to do.
This activity lets children be in control of the materials.

Level 1

At first, children get involved in exploring the flat surface of the piece of paper or cardboard on which the collage will be made. They begin by placing scraps of paper or material on the paper without any plan. They use the scraps as they find them and do not cut or tear them to change them into any special shape.

After exploring the surface in a random way, they want to glue the pieces to the surface. Young children are often unable to control the flow of the glue or the amount of paste taken from the jar, so this stage can get very messy. In pasting pieces onto the surface, children rarely overlap them. At first, they use only a few scraps to make the collage. Some collages may contain only one or two pieces of paper or material. With experience, children begin to use more and more objects as part of their collages.

Level 2

Children spend more time making their collages. They can better control how much glue or paste they want to use. They also begin to change the pieces of material to the size or shape they want.

Children pay particular attention to the careful selection of the "right" piece of material. It may be the right color or the right texture. It may be a shiny piece of tin foil. Children will search through the entire collection of material scraps to find the one piece they want.

Once found, that piece is glued to the surface. Then they resume the search for the next "right" piece, and glue that one to the surface. They repeat this process until the collage is finished. Now the collage starts to include pieces placed partially on top of each other. Overlapping is typical of this level. Also, children begin to make collages that are not flat.

Throughout this process of hunt, paste, and hunt again, children talk about what they are doing, what they are looking for, and what they have found. Their talk is most likely to be thinking out loud rather than conversation. Unless a child asks a specific question, a parent probably need not respond to the child's comments.

Children often indicate that they have finished making their collages by calling the finished product a house or a particular

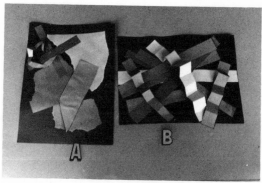

Collages with overlapping pieces

person. This naming process comes after the fact. Rarely has the child planned what has turned out.

Level 3

Collages made at this level involve much overlapping of materials. Many children try to build up from the flat surface. They may glue a toilet paper roll on its edge or paste a crumpled piece of paper to the flat surface. Some will even paste material on top of the toilet paper roll. This is an example of exploring vertical space.

Children explore another type of space by decorating the inside of the toilet paper roll or paper cup which they have glued to the surface. They attempt this after they glue the object to the surface, making the task more difficult.

After much exploration of the flat surface, vertical space, and space inside of objects, children are ready to plan their collages. They usually create a mental picture of what their collage will look like. This may be a design or a picture representing a real thing such as a house. Then children select the right material. If the right piece is not there, they cut a piece from a large piece or use two small pieces to make one of the right size. Children know what they need to make their planned collages and will find some material to meet their needs.

Some children select all the pieces needed before beginning. Others paste the pieces on the paper as they go along, but they do place the pieces on the paper according to their plan.

At this level, children often announce beforehand what

they are going to make. They want to tell you all the details about the product being made as well as the process they are using. They invent stories about what they have made and how they made it.

It is important that parents show interest in their children's work. You might comment on the bright colors or interesting design they used. You might also mention how hard they worked. Hanging up their work for all to see will encourage them to make more.

Possible Learning Outcomes

Ideas and Their Vocabulary
Place words: on, under, on top of, up
Quantitative words: many, few, more, less

Thinking Skills
Classifying: putting objects together by types of material, size, color, or shape
Planning: thinking up a design, getting the materials, and following through on the design

Symbolic Representation
Scraps of material are thought of as a house, boat, tree, or school

Estimation
Estimating amounts: glue needed to paste one piece of material
Estimating area: finding or making a piece of material the right size for a certain space

Perceptual-motor Skills
Eye-hand coordination: cutting and tearing materials or paper
Visual discrimination: selecting materials that look alike or different in color, size, texture, shape
Visual imagery: forming a mental picture of the scene to be made enables the child to plan the collage

ALTERNATE MATERIALS
Any and all scraps of materials, such as paper or wood, that you want to get rid of. Place these in a box so that the children can find them easily.

2.3 Dress-ups

MATERIALS

Parents' clothing and shoes
Accessories such as pipe, handbag, briefcase, hat, jewelry
Make-up
A place to keep these things

DESCRIPTION

Children like to dress up in their parent's clothing and play mommy and daddy. You should encourage such activities. Dress-ups let children act out adult roles and help them understand what it is that people do and how they do it. Often this play shows that the children have misconceptions about how the world works. Observing children in such play allows parents to see the world as their children see it.

Children need a space of their own where they can keep their dress-up things. Since children often play dress-up with a friend, they need props for at least two people.

Level 1

Very young children need few props. Just a hat and a bag (a handbag or briefcase) help them to become somebody else. During a single playtime the person they are pretending to be may change. They may start out being mommy, then become teacher, and then doctor. The handbag changes from being mommy's handbag to teacher's book bag to the doctor's bag. Such changes occur as children act out the roles of the people they know.

The stories they act out usually involve simple plots about something they have experienced. A trip to the store, taking care

Children like to act out different roles.

of a baby, or visiting relatives are typical events. Both boys and girls usually show their gentle, caring nature as they pretend to take care of someone else in the same way they want to be taken care of.

The props do not play a major part in the dramatic play. It is the setting up of the situation, deciding how to do something, and talking about what is happening that is the heart of dress-ups. The props may prompt the play, but the true value lies in acting out different roles and situations.

Level 2

Older children make their dress-ups more like the real world. No longer will just a hat and bag do. Having the right shoes, blouse, and jewelry becomes important. They spend more time and attention on dressing for the part. The play itself becomes longer and more involved. Children create many new interesting situations to act out. For them, going to the store now involves shopping for a party and getting all the different things they need to prepare for a party. They may prepare a list and check things off as they are bought and paid for. After shopping, they go home and prepare for the party. Children use whatever props are handy to represent whatever it is that they need. Their story is played out from beginning to end, and their plots — unlike those of youger children — often do not change during their play.

In another type of dramatic play, children may pretend to

be television or movie characters. Such acting out is healthy and can help children learn the difference between what is real and what is pretend. A towel can become Superman's cape or a magic carpet. But children cannot fly and parents need to help children come to terms with reality and make-believe. You may ask children if real people can fly or if certain fantastic events can happen in everyday life in order to protect them from hurting themselves as they try to act out a role they may believe is true.

POSSIBLE LEARNING OUTCOMES

Language Development
Oral communication skills (see page 27) improve as children talk with each other

Thinking Skills
Modeling the real world: creating a situation and acting out the events; answering the question "What do people do in this situation?"

Symbolic Representation
Using an object to be something else: a handbag becomes a book bag, doctor's bag, or briefcase
Clarifying roles: identifying the correct functions of a job (doctor, police officer) or of a place (grocery store, bus)
Creative thinking involved in developing fantasy action in an imaginary world

Perceptual-motor Skills
Visual imagery: forming a mental picture of a doctor's office enables the child to plan the fantasy

ALTERNATE MATERIALS
Children need many different kinds of clothes, hats, shoes, and other props which they can wear to become whomever they want. By putting aside a collection of such things in a place where the children can get at it, parents are encouraging children to engage in dramatic play. Also, such a collection makes it easier for parents to insist that children do not use new clothes or shoes.

2.4 Food Preparation

MATERIALS
>   Measuring cups, spoons (regular and long-handled), mixing
>   bowls, pot to boil water
>   Ingredients listed in recipes
>   Recipes printed on cards

DESCRIPTION
Preparing food can be fun for children. Such shared experiences can be valuable for both children and their parents. However, children will want to continue to help in food preparation only if the first few experiences are successful.

It is important that the first few times you have your children help you prepare food that you keep the recipes simple. It helps to have a copy of the recipe printed on a card and available for the children to see even if they cannot read it. Another way of helping a child who does not yet read is to make a recipe card using pictures in place of many of the words.

When children work and play in the kitchen, be concerned for safety. You must supervise your children in almost all food preparation activities. A major area of danger is the stove or oven. When handling hot things, it may be necessary for the children to observe rather than handle the material. One way in which food preparation is beneficial is that it helps children learn to use tools properly. This means that you need to tell children some safety rules and expect them to follow them. For example, you must stress proper handling of knives, glassware, and electrical appliances. Also, children need to work on surfaces of the right height. This may mean standing on a chair or stool so they can work on the kitchen counter or table. Again, you must watch them to make sure they are careful.

J & I TRAIL MIX

3/4 cup peanuts
  1 cup sunflower seeds
1/2 cup mixed nuts
1/2 cup carob chips
  1 cup raisins
  1 cup mixed dried fruit

The recipe can be made with nuts and sunflower seeds that are either roasted, raw, salted, or unsalted. The mixed dried fruit can be toasted coconut shreds, dried dates, dried banana chips, or any other available dried fruit.

In order to make children's first tries at making J & I Trail Mix successful, we suggest that you premix all the ingredients except the carob chips. Have the mixed ingredients in a bowl and the measuring cup and carob chips on the counter. Show the children the "1/2 cup carob chips" on the recipe card and show them the "1/2" written on the measuring cup. Tell them that they must fill the cup with chips up to the 1/2 mark. You may want to hold the measuring cup while the children place spoonfuls of carob chips into the cup. Ask the children if there are enough chips in the cup. Show them you read a measuring cup by putting the 1/2 mark at eye level and seeing if the chips are at that line.

When there is 1/2 cup of chips, put the rest of the chips away. Then place the rest of the ingredients directly in front of the children. Now the children are ready to mix in the carob chips. Have them pour some chips into the mix and then stir them into the rest of the ingredients. Repeat this until all the chips are used and the mix is throughly stirred. Then place most of the mixture into a closed, airtight container. Leave the rest out to be eaten.

When the children can do the above easily, have them put two ingredients into the mixture. Show them these ingredients on the recipe card. Eventually, they will be able to start from the very beginning and mix all six ingredients in the recipe. Be certain to have them stir the ingredients together after each new one is added.

You can have the children select a right-sized bowl in which to make the trail mix. This may mean that they will select too small a bowl and then more than one mixing bowl will need to be washed. With practice they will select the right-sized bowl.

JELLO

1 package of Jello	The recipe for Jello can be ex-
1 cup boiling water	panded to include pieces of fresh
1 cup cold water	or canned fruit.

Making Jello is a short, quick, simple food preparation task. You begin by boiling some water. Have the children empty the entire package of Jello into a mixing bowl. After the water has come to a boil, carefully measure out 1 cup of boiling water. Slowly pour the entire cup into the mixing bowl, making certain that the water does not splash. Now children may help by stirring the water into the Jello. Have them stir until all the Jello is mixed with the water. Point out any of the powder that is still not dissolved. Ask them to keep stirring until all the Jello is dissolved.

> **Caution:** In allowing children to work with or near very hot water, you must take care that they understand that the water will burn them if they touch it and that they have sufficient coordination not to splash or spill it on themselves when they stir it.

When that is done, have them measure 1 cup of cold water. Again, be certain that they read the measuring cup from the outside. Have them carefully pour the cold water into the mixture. Again have them stir the mixture.

Tell them to keep the Jello on the counter until it has cooled to room temperature. You can show them how to check the Jello's temperature by touching the side of the mixing bowl. When cooled to room temperature, about 30 minutes, the Jello can be placed in the refrigerator.

While waiting for the Jello to cool, use that time to clean up. Ask children to help wash or dry the utensils used.

Older children will be able to make both these recipes with little assistance. They will be able to find and take out all the ingredients and utensils called for in the recipe. You can also expect them to follow the steps in the recipe from beginning to end.

POSSIBLE LEARNING OUTCOMES
    Ideas and Their Vocabulary
        Process words: stir, dissolve, mix
        Names of ingredients
        Quantitative words: 1/2 cup, more, less, 1 cup
        Temperature words: hot, cool, cold

    Language Development
        "Learning to read": matching printed words or mathematical symbols on recipe cards with the same symbols on boxes and measuring cup

Thinking Skills
> Nature of substances: transformation of form from powder to liquid to solid
> Planning: deciding what is needed and getting these items
> Order of events: combining ingredients in proper order (cold water used first will not work)
> Locating needed ingredients and utensils

Measurement
> Volume: reading a measuring cup

Estimation
> Estimating volume by selecting the right size bowl

ALTERNATE MATERIALS
> Other simple recipes such as pudding, oatmeal, powdered milk or rice can be used.

ADDITIONAL RESOURCES
> There are many cookbooks available for children. The following are but a few of them. You may want to check your local library for other children's cookbooks.

Barnett, P., and Dalton, R. *The Kid's Cookbook.* Concord. Cal.: Nitty Gritty Publishing Co., 1973.

Copper, J. *Love at First Bite.* New York: Alfred A. Knopf, Inc., 1977.

Croft, K. *The Good For Me Cookbook.* San Francisco: R. and E. Associates, 1971.

Johnson, G., and Povey, G. *Metric Milk Shakes and Witches Cakes.* New York: Scholastic, 1976.

Lenley, V., and Lenley, L. *Children's Cookery Naturally.* Cave Junction, Ore.: Wilderness House, 1980.

Parent's Nursery School. *Kids Are Natural Cooks.* Boston: Houghton-Mifflin, 1974.

Stangl, J. *The No-Cook Cookery Cookbook.* Camarillo, Cal.: 1979.

2.5 Making Lunch for a Friend

MATERIALS
>Table and chairs
>Dishes, eating utensils
>Something to be the pretend food

DESCRIPTION
>Children often make pretend meals for real or imaginary friends. Some of the things that they do in such situations include setting the table, preparing the food, and eating it.

>During such pretend activities, children like to talk a lot. They talk about what they are doing and what they are going to do, as well as have a general conversation with their friends. Much of the learning from this activity comes from the talking the children do. Pretending or imagining also makes major contributions to their store of knowledge.

Level 1
Very young children usually talk about what is around them. They tell their friend, real or imaginary, about what they have in their table setting, the food they are making, and how good or bad the food tastes, whether the food is real or not.

When pretending, children give directions and like to control the situation. Often the place in which the lunch is being eaten changes from the home to a restaurant. Children do not care that they have made this change in place. The time spent in such a pretend meal is often very short.

Level 2
As children get older and have more experiences, their fantasy meal becomes more like a real meal. It takes more time and becomes more complex. The place of the meal often remains the same throughout the fantasy. The conversation is more closely modeled after that of the real world, whether the conversation is with the waitress or about the food. More people, pretend and/or real, are included in this play situation.

As children's fantasies become longer and more elaborate,

their conversations become longer and more complex. Their sentences are also much longer and they try out new words, which are often misused because their meanings are not yet clear to the children.

Children are better able to share the control of the play with a real friend. They attempt to have a grown-up conversation. If the playmate is a pretend friend, the child tries to express that other person's point of view, even if it differs from theirs.

Level 3

Eventually, if you encourage your children to play-act, they can create complicated fantasy meals in which many friends and activities are involved. Several conversations can be taking place at this imaginary meal, and the time spent at the event can be quite long.

Lunch being served by a waiter

At all three levels children do not need real food or table settings to have a pretend lunch. They may use a top of a box for a plate and a scrap of paper for the food. Older children may draw or make something that looks like what it is supposed to be. A sandwich may be two cards with a piece of paper in between. This models the two slices of bread and slice of food that make up a real sandwich.

It does not matter to the children that they do not have real dishes and food. In fact, there is more to learn from pretending and imagining the dishes and food than from using the real things. Creating and acting out the fantasy is what the children are enjoying.

Language Development
Oral communication skills (see page 27) improve as children talk with each other.

Thinking Skills
Planning: deciding what is needed for a pretend meal and using symbolic representation (see below), where necessary, to act out the event

Modeling the real world: creating a situation and acting out the events; answering the question "What do people do in this situation?"

Acting out roles: behaving as they think a waiter does behave.

Symbolic Representation
Symbolizing: using pieces of paper as a sandwich

Perceptual-motor Skills
Visual imagery: forming a mental picture of a meal with a friend enables the child to plan the pretend meal

ALTERNATE MATERIALS
Any and all things children can get their hands on. Dolls become people; paper becomes food; a book becomes a menu.

2.6 Modeling Materials

MATERIALS
Commercial Play-Doh® or ingredients listed in the recipe below

Wax paper, cardboard, or old cookie sheet

Airtight container for storage

DESCRIPTION

Modeling activities, using Play-Doh® or similar materials, are among children's favorites. These activities allow children freedom in deciding how to use the materials. Children find these activities relaxing. At the same time, the materials give children many chances to use their imagination and creativity.

Parents can buy materials such as Play-Doh® or make a home-made version, with or without children's help, using the recipes listed below.

When using modeling materials, it is helpful and neater to give children a special work place. A piece of cardboard, a large sheet of wax paper, or an old cookie sheet make an excellent work surface.

Recipe

1 cup flour	
1/2 cup salt	Add a few drops of food coloring
1/3 cup water	to the water. Knead ingredients
1 Tbs. cooking oil	together until smooth. Refrigerate
Food coloring	in airtight container.

Level 1

Children's first response to modeling material is to explore it. They push it, pull it, roll it, squeeze it, and bang it. They make balls out of it, roll it into a snake, and squash it into a pancake. All this exploration is a necessary part of their play and probably will last a very long time. This is the only way they can learn how the material works.

Level 2

After "messing about" with the modeling materials, children try to make something that looks like something they know. They may try to make a person, a cat, or a birthday cake. They are usually successful with the birthday cake because it is flat. If they try to make a person with just a head and a body by putting one ball on top of another, there is no problem. However, once they try to put arms, legs or a tail on a figure they have difficulty.

Their attempts to put a tail onto a figure by making one and sticking it onto the body usually do not work. They will try dif-

A. Cat's ears have been pulled out of the clay in the head.
B. Elephant's trunk and ears were attached; one ear fell off. Note the macaroni eyes.

ferent ways of doing this before asking for help. Only after they have asked for help should you show them a better way of making a tail by pulling the materials from the body rather than sticking an extra piece of material onto the body.

It usually takes children a long time to believe that using one big piece of clay is sometimes the best way to make something with arms, legs, or a tail. Part of the delay comes from their inability to handle physically the modeling material and make it do a particular thing. Such careful manipulation of a modeling material often gets in the way of playing with it. Making something may become a task rather than play.

Level 3

In time, children find that making the object is as much fun as playing with the modeling materials. As they are better able to manipulate the materials, the objects look more and more like what they are trying to make.

At this level, children can make such things as animals, houses, people, and cars. They use a combination of techniques that they have learned during the "messing about" stage. They still, though, enjoy doing all the things they did at Level 1.

After the "messing about" stage, children's play with modeling materials can be enhanced by the use of such things as: popsicle sticks, cookie cutters, straws, toothpicks, macaroni, and many other small, safe materials. Having such things handy for children is desirable but not absolutely necessary. Sometimes they will use these things, and then the very next time ignore them.

POSSIBLE LEARNING OUTCOMES

Ideas and Their Vocabulary
Names of colors: red, green
Names of textures: smooth, rough, crinkly
Place words: on top of, beside
Quantitative words: a lot, a little
Names of shapes: round, flat

Thinking Skills
Nature of modeling materials: pliable, easily changes form
Planning: thinking up a design for a house and carrying through on that design
Figuring out how to best make arms and legs on a figure by either adding more material or manipulating the material that is already there

Symbolic Representation
Symbolizing: using the molded object as the thing it was made to be, such as a car, house, or cat

Measurement
Conservation of mass: changing the shape of a piece of modeling material or dividing it into several smaller pieces does not change the total amount of material

Estimation
Estimating amounts: modeling material needed to fill a cookie cutter or to make a house

Perceptual-motor Skills
Visual imagery: forming a mental picture of a dog enables the child to make a dog

ALTERNATE MATERIALS
Clay, plasticine, mud, wet sand

2.7 Playing in the Bathtub

MATERIALS

Plastic containers with lids of assorted sizes and shapes

Squeeze bottles

Plastic funnels

Plastic measuring cups

Bath tray, string bag, or bucket to hold everything

DESCRIPTION

Playing with water is fun for children. Whether a puddle or the ocean, water can hold children's attention for long periods of time. Children have many opportunities for learning different things as they play with water and watch what happens when they play with things in the water.

The bathtub is the best place for children to play with water. Here the amount of water and its temperature are controllable. With the water confined to a specific place, the tub, no great damage can be caused by water splashed outside it. Water play can also take place in the kitchen or utility room.

Level 1

Children use themselves to explore the water in the bathtub. They splash and slide around in the tub. Children take great delight in making waves, but is is not necessary for the waves to become so big that you wind up with more water outside the tub than inside it. You need to allow children some freedom but you also must set limits as to the amount of splashing they may do. Sometimes in sliding around the tub a child's head may go under the water. This may scare the child and you should provide the necessary comfort while the child is still in the tub.

Children like to play with things while in the tub. A collection of plastic containers with tops, squeeze bottles, and measuring cups are all that is necessary for endless hours of play. The more sizes and shapes in the collection the better.

At first, children simply fill a container and then empty it by pouring out the water, often from a position above their heads. They are fascinated with the waterfall that they have created. They repeat this many times using many different containers. Eventually, they also pour water back and forth from one container to another. They particularly enjoy pouring water from a larger container to a smaller one because they enjoy watching the water overflow the smaller container.

Children watch the containers float on the water and enjoy sinking them by pushing them to the bottom of the tub. Often the container bobs up to the surface only to be pushed down again. Children see that most soaps and a wash cloth do not float. At this level, children are unable to understand why some things float and some things don't.

Children also enjoy using squeeze bottles as water guns to shoot the water against the wall. They attempt to shoot the water as far as possible. They are not ready to understand why the water goes a given distance. Once again, their explorations and play are attempts to understand why things happen.

Level 2

Older children use the same materials and do the same things as those described in Level 1. But now their play is more elaborate. They talk about what they are doing and make up stories using the containers as boats, dishes, or food.

They also spend a lot of time lining up the containers along the edge of the tub. At first they pay no attention to the size or shape of the bottle. Later they may arrange things by shape or by size order. Now, in addition to making a smaller container overflow by pouring water into it from a larger container, they may also use one smaller container, several times, to fill a large container.

The strange shapes of some containers fool them. They are often surprised that a short, wide container actually holds more water than a taller, thin container.

At this level children ask many questions about what's happening. They want to know why some containers float and some sink or why water overflows the container. You can answer these questions in different ways. For example, a piece of soap sinks because it is heavier than the water. You probably need to tell children this. On the other hand, you can show children that filling an empty container makes it so heavy that instead of floating, it sinks.

Parents need to know that there is no one way to answer children's questions. Sometimes you tell them, sometimes you show them, sometimes you ask them another question, and sometimes you admit that you do not know.

Level 3

Children still enjoy using the same materials in their water play. The stories they create are longer and more involved, and have a beginning, a middle, and an end.

They are beginning to understand the answers to the questions they asked in Level 2. Over and over again, they test their theories as to why things happen. If they think they can make the water shoot a greater distance by pushing hard on a squeeze bottle, they will test this theory. First they squeeze the bottle a little and watch how far the water shoots. Then they squeeze the bottle a little harder, and the water shoots a little farther.

After checking this out several times, they share this knowledge with you. They may ask, "Do you know why the water shoots out of the bottle?" and then proceed to tell you while showing you. Their answers are often incomplete. They probably do not understand how the amount of water in the bottle influences how far the water shoots. This is because they only understand what they can see and simply ignore information which does not fit into their scheme of things.

Whenever children play in the tub, they should be expected to empty all containers and put them away. In addition to learning to put things away when they are done with them, they are also learning how different arrangements of the same things can take up more or less space.

POSSIBLE LEARNING OUTCOMES

Ideas and Their Vocabulary
Place words: into, onto, out, underneath, on top of
Quantitative and comparative words: bigger/smaller, more/less, full/empty/partially filled, heavier/lighter

Thinking Skills
Classifying: determining which objects float and which sink; which containers are full and which empty
Seriation: putting containers in size order largest to smallest and smallest to largest

Measurement
Measuring volume by counting how many times a full, small container is used to fill a larger container

Perceptual-motor Skills
Eye-hand coordination: pouring the water back and forth between containers, squirting water from squeeze bottles

ALTERNATE MATERIALS
Kitchen or utility room sink, a large tub of water, or a wading pool

2.8   Playing with Blocks

MATERIALS
One set of unit blocks with:
at least 50 blocks
a minimum of 8 different shapes

DESCRIPTION
Playing with blocks is an activity that holds most children's interest even as they get older. Children can build with many different things. Shoe boxes, cardboard or foam blocks, and wooden unit blocks are only a few of the things that can be used. What is important to the children is that these things can be put together to make something. Building is fun, and no two building experiences need be the same.

Wooden unit blocks are highly durable. In comparison with other toys, they are inexpensive. Also, a basic set can be added to easily by purchasing additional sets. This plaything can grow in complexity as children grow.

More learning is possible from blocks than from any other plaything. This learning will help children when they learn to read, do math, and solve problems. Because there are no rules, no "right way" or specific purpose to playing with blocks, children are free to make any kind of structure they want. This freedom to create is what makes block play so much fun for children as well as so imprtant to their intellectual growth. This is why we strongly recommend that every child be provided with the tools for playing with blocks.

Level 1

Children's first play with blocks involves moving them from one place to another and stacking or making piles of blocks. Through this play they learn which blocks are best for building towers and whether to place blocks flat or on edge. By repeating this kind of play they not only gain knowledge of the blocks but also develop skill in handling them.

At this level, their structures are simple. They tend to be low and spread-out, like roads or simple towers. The fun comes from handling the blocks and from repeating skills that they have already mastered.

Level 2

Once they can build simple towers, children often build two towers next to each other and try to connect them by placing a block from the top of one tower to another tower. This is called bridging. Children need considerable practice over a long period of time before they become skillful at bridging. They have difficulty in judging the distance between the towers and in selecting the right block to make the bridge.

Children also begin to make longer roads. Eventually the

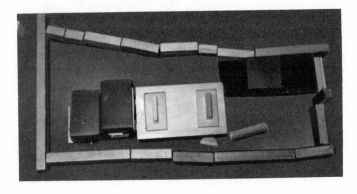

An object enclosed in a space

Repeated pattern of two
blocks bridged by a third

end of the road comes back to the starting point, creating an enclosed space. Children often make such an enclosed space accidentally. Once they have discovered how to do this, they make many different sizes and shapes of enclosed spaces. They often try to build a space around something, including themselves, thereby enclosing an object in space.

Throughout Level 2 children are primarily interested in building for the sake of building. It is the activity that is important to them. They also repeat their play over and over again. In this way they practice their newly found skills until they feel that they have mastered them.

Level 3

After mastering the art of bridging and making enclosed spaces, children begin to make higher structures in a more confined area. They also begin to make decorative patterns with the blocks. These designs come from the repetition of a small structure made with a few blocks. Such a structure may be two small blocks bridged by a third. This pattern is repeated along the road they build at the base of the building. Children often end up with a structure which looks very involved but actually resulted from the repetition of one or two designs.

At this time, children want to know the names of the different shapes of the blocks in the set. They also tend to name the building they have finished, calling it a school or a house.

Level 4

Once children have mastered the skills in Level 3, they begin to make buildings that look like buildings they have seen. They set out to build houses, schools, or farms. They use these buildings as part of the stories they are creating or the games they are playing.

Older children tend to plan out the details of their construction in advance. They announce that they will be building a school and plan out the design in their heads before beginning to build. When they play with a friend, they will discuss these plans and possibly assign tasks. They usually decide to build a particular building because it plays a role in a story or game that they want to play.

All levels of block play involve repetition. Children enjoy redoing activities that have been successful ones for them. In each higher level of block play, children use the skills of the lower levels. Children will continue to enjoy playing with blocks throughout their elementary school years.

POSSIBLE LEARNING OUTCOMES

Ideas and Their Vocabulary
Names of shapes: arc, long rectangle, cube, square
Names of buildings: school, store, house
Place words: on top of, next to, below, inside
Quantitative words: as many as, number names (four)
Comparative words: bigger/smaller, longer/shorter, same size as

Number Ideas
One-to-one correspondence: placing one block on each side of the door
Many-to-one correspondence: two-to-one correspondence — two small blocks are as long as one big block
Counting: the number of blocks in a tower or needed for a road
Cardinality: "threeness," knowing three blocks are being used, no matter what size or shape they are

Idea of a fraction: if four blocks of the same size and shape make a square, then each is one fourth of the square

Thinking Skills
Nature of blocks: it is easier to stack them flat than on edge; non-flexible — cannot change direction in middle of block, blocks do not bend
Classifying: putting blocks together by size and shape
Planning: deciding what blocks will be needed to build something, getting these, and following through on the plan for the building
Patterning: creating a pattern and repeating it in the construction

Measurement
Measuring length by using one block as a unit and counting how many blocks are in a row
Measuring perimeter by counting the number of blocks of one size that are in a row around an object
Measuring area by counting the number of blocks of one size that are needed to fill in an enclosed, flat space
Estimation
Estimating length by deciding how far apart to put two blocks that are to be bridged with a third block

Perceptual-motor Skills
Eye-hand coordination: stacking blocks and bridging
Directionality: following a road from the beginning to end with a toy car; changing direction in a road when needed
Visual discrimination: selecting blocks that look alike or different in size, shape, or both
Visual imagery: forming a mental picture of a school building enables the child to plan the building

ALTERNATE MATERIALS
Though many different materials such as shoe boxes or cardboard blocks can be used for block play, these are not as valuable

to the children's development as wooden unit blocks. Non-wooden blocks are lighter, do not have the variety in shape or size, and are less durable than wooden unit blocks. They are, though, considerably less expensive.

A beginning set of unit blocks can be supplemented over time with more advanced sets available from the manufacturers. Such sets include blocks of different shapes and sizes as well as more blocks of the basic shapes and sizes.

For alternate building toys, read the section on construction toys in Chapter 6.

2.9   Pots 'n' Pans

MATERIALS
>   An assortment of pots and pans with lids
>   Cookie sheets
>   Colanders
>   Nesting plastic or aluminum mixing bowls

DESCRIPTION
>   Children get considerable pleasure out of emptying the kitchen cabinet that holds the things used for cooking. After emptying out all the pots 'n' pans, they enjoy playing with them.

> **Caution:** In allowing children to explore cabinets containing pots 'n' pans, you must take care that glass pots and other items that can break are not included among those things with which the children are allowed to play.

Level 1
Children's play often involves spreading out the pots 'n' pans in a line, stacking them, or putting them one inside another. They usually do this without paying too much attention to the size of things. Children may spend a lot of time trying to fit a

large pot into a smaller one. They also see nothing wrong with placing a very large lid on top of a relatively small pan. Also the noise that comes from banging the pots against each other or something else makes playing with the metal objects more fun than playing with plastic objects such as mixing bowls.

Very young children cannot be expected to fit all the pots 'n' pans back into the closet. They simply do not understand the size relationships among the pots so that they can fit one inside the other, nor do they understand spatial relationships in order to fit all the pots 'n' pans into a given space.

Level 2

While playing with the pots 'n' pans on the floor, children often make piles of objects by shape. The cookie sheets and other rectangular objects go in one pile. The frying pan and other round, shallow objects go in another pile. The saucepans go in yet another pile. Children often make up rules based on the size of the objects. Therefore, they may put the small frying pan and small saucepans together, the dutch oven and large frying pans together, or big pots such as spaghetti pots or soup pots together.

As they do this sorting, children may ask for the names of the things they are sorting. You should tell them the proper names for each item. That is how they learn such words as colander, strainer, and frying pan. They also learn that there may be two names for the same thing; we use both "lid" and "cover" for the object which goes on top of a pot.

With older children, the order relationship among the pots 'n' pans begins to make sense. Using a trial and error approach, they now can match the right lid with its pot or pan. They also begin to make towers with the pans by turning them upside down; they can then place a smaller pan on top of a larger pan. At first, they leave some pans out of the tower. Eventually, they make as tall a tower as possible by placing these pans in strict size order. This is called seriation.

They also seriate objects by nesting, that is, placing pots, pans, or mixing bowls one inside another. Again, their first attempts are trial and error and they do not use all the pieces in the set. Eventually, they place the items in strict size order using all pots, pans, or bowls that are available in the set.

At this level, children often line up the items on the floor.

Seriation: A tower of pots

They place them in size order from largest to smallest or smallest to largest. They also line up the lids in size order without matching the lid to its proper pan. After much practice with this, they double seriate. This means that they line up the pots and pans as well as the lids, matching each pot or pan with its own lid. You might reinforce this by asking them to find the lid for the pan you are using in cooking.

Once they have begun to gain skill at nesting the pots 'n' pans, you can expect them to be more able to put everything back into the cabinet. They may still have trouble doing this, for they cannot see how the handles of frying pans can be turned so that they are out of the way. Their attempts to replace the pots 'n' pans, and moving them around on the shelves of the cabinets, are good learning experiences for them.

Level 3
The children at this level can easily nest the pots 'n' pans. They delight in making very tall towers by using not only the pots from one set but by also using cookie sheets, mixing bowls, and other objects which they balance precariously on the top of the tower.

They are also able to help you empty the dish drainer and put the pots 'n' pans away, for they easily see the size relationships among the pots 'n' pans. Their sense of spatial relationships has been greatly refined and they are better able to move things around so that they can place all the pots 'n' pans on the available shelves.

POSSIBLE LEARNING OUTCOMES

Ideas and Their Vocabulary
Names of pots and pans: saucepan, frying pan
Comparative words: large/medium/small, bigger/littler

Language Development
Two names for the same object: lid and cover, skillet and pan

Number Ideas
One-to-one correspondence: matching one pot to its lid
Counting the number of pots in a tower

Thinking Skills
Nature of materials: plastic objects make less noise when dropped than do metal objects
Classifying: putting pots 'n' pans together by shape, size, with lids or without lids; using two factors at one time (size and depth, size and material)
Seriation: putting pots in size order, largest to smallest or smallest to largest
Double-seriation: matching two sets of objects according to size, such as matching a set of pots with their lids

Perceptual-motor Skills
Eye-hand coordination: stacking pots one on top of another; putting away pots

ALTERNATE MATERIALS
Plastic or other nonbreakable dishes
Flatware (knives, forks, spoons)

2.10 Sewing

MATERIALS
> Blunt-point needles
> Scissors
> Yarn and thread
> Buttons
> Cotton or pieces of foam
> Small pieces of felt and scraps of other materials

DESCRIPTION

Sewing is a survival skill which all children should learn. It can be fun and also gives them a chance to do the kind of things adults do. It can, though, be frustrating to children if they are asked to work with materials for which they are not ready.

Sewing differs from most of the activities in this book in that children often want to make something by sewing. Therefore, the joy comes not from just doing the activity but also from what is made.

Level 1

If children want to sew when you sew, it is best to give them blunt-point needles, threaded with yarn which has a knot at the end, and a scrap of material of a color different from the yarn. It is important that they be able to see the thread on the material. Children begin by making stitches in the middle of the scrap of material. These may or may not cross each other. At this level, there is no pattern.

After repeating this activity many times, children will try to sew two scraps of material together. They simply place one piece on top of the other and make the same kind of random stitching they used on one piece of material. Their next attempts will have them overlapping only parts of the scraps and making stitches only on the overlapped parts. Often they miss and stray stitches wind up on both scraps. With practice they are able to control their sewing so that the stitches are only on the overlapped material.

Level 2

Children who have mastered the skills of Level 1 often try

to sew the scraps together with as little overlap as possible. This leads them to try to put the scraps one on top of the other with one edge matching another. They then stitch along the edge as close to the edge as possible. It sometimes helps if you use a marker to draw a path along which they are to sew.

At this point, you may want to show them how to stitch over the edge instead of along the edge. After seeing this overlapping stitch, they usually sew a border all around the scrap while practicing. With practice, the stitches become more uniform in size and spacing.

Level 3

Having gained the skills at Level 2, children are ready to try to make a pin cushion or small pillow. These both involve sewing together two scraps of material of the same size, about three fourths of the way around. If you cut several such scraps of material for them, they can pick the ones they like.

After using an overlapping stitch to sew about three fourths of the way around, leaving the threaded needle attached, it is necessary to stuff the item with either cotton or foam. Children can do the stuffing but you may need to stop them from overstuffing the item. If too much is put inside, they will be unable to put together the final edges of the cushion. After matching up the last edges, they can sew them together with an overlapping stitch.

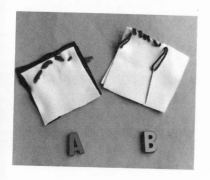

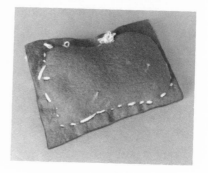

A: Scraps of materials that are overlapped

B: An overlapping stitch

A pincushion made by a four-year-old

Level 4

Once children can make pin cushions and a small pillow from materials you have prepared, they are ready to do the preparation by themselves. They can draw a picture of the size of the pin cushion or pillow they wish to make. They need to be shown that by doubling the material they will only need to cut around the pattern once to get two matching pieces. (For some children cutting the doubled material may be difficult.) They can select the color yarn they want to use. After making their plans and preparing the material, they are ready to practice their pillow-making skills.

Older children become interested in decorating the cushion. This may involve sewing buttons or small pieces of material onto the cushion. This work takes even greater manual dexterity than the other work and may frustrate children. It will help them if you supply buttons with large holes to ease this task. Soon they discover that it is much easier to decorate one side of the material before stuffing the cushion and sewing it together. Children often make very elaborate designs on the cushion.

POSSIBLE LEARNING OUTCOMES

Ideas and Their Vocabulary

Names of materials: satin, felt, cotton, cloth
Names of tools: needle, thread, scissors

Thinking Skills

Planning: thinking up a design, getting the materials, and following through on the design
Order of Events: deciding what should be done first (cut material), then second (sew about 3/4 the way around), and so forth

Estimation

Estimating length by cutting a piece of thread thought to be the right length to sew the cushion
Estimating volume by guessing right amount of stuffing to fill a cushion

Perceptual-motor Skills
Eye-hand coordination: threading the needle, stitching a straight line, following a design
Directionality: directing the needle when sewing around an object

ALTERNATE MATERIALS
Many different kinds of materials can be sewn. Even styrofoam trays (like those used for packaging meat in the food store) become a piece of material that can be stitched. Older children enjoying stitching around the edge, thereby making a picture frame.

Various items can be used to decorate the objects made. These include buttons, sequins, and pieces of ribbons
Commercial sewing cards can be purchased.

2.11   Stringing Activities

MATERIALS
Assortment of beads, two or more kinds of macaroni
Yarn or long shoe laces

DESCRIPTION
Children enjoy making necklaces and belts out of some of the strangest things. Given a piece of yarn and some beads, they willingly spend long periods of time making things to wear. These stringing activities give children many opportunities to develop skills important to their future learning.

Level 1
Given some yarn and a collection of beads and macaroni, young children will spend time stringing the beads and macaroni. They do this because it is fun to put things on a piece of yarn and then take them off the yarn. They do this over and over again.

Usually children select either the beads or the macaroni to play with. After stringing all beads, they may string the macaroni onto the same piece of yarn or they may use a separate piece of yarn. This sorting of the materials is their way of organizing their play. Some children may fill the entire string with objects. Others may leave the string partially empty.

If the yarn does not have a big enough knot at its end, the objects slide off the yarn. Children often enoy watching a bead that they have placed on one end slide down the yarn and onto the table. They like to hold up the yarn so that the bead gains speed as it goes down the yarn.

But if children are trying to keep the beads on the yarn, it can be frustrating if there is not a large enough knot at the end of the piece of yarn. They are not easily able to hold in one hand both unknotted ends of a piece of yarn with beads on it. To help them get the most out of these stringing activities, most pieces of yarn should have large knots on one end. This lets the children decide whether they want the beads to stay on the string.

Another problem that can occur when children are using yarn is for the ends of the yarn to unravel. Taping or gluing the ends of the yarn will help the children to string the beads easily.

Level 2

After practice at stringing and unstringing beads and macaroni, children begin to plan what to put on the yarn. Now they think of what they are making as necklaces, bracelets, or belts.

If children decide to work with just beads, they may choose only one color before using a second color. Or, they may decide to alternate colors, using only two. They may make a necklace with red and blue beads, alternating colors. After many experiences using two colors, they then may use three or more colors.

If children choose to work with macaroni they will develop similar patterns. They may string one kind of macaroni at a time, such as all chariot wheels, then all ziti. Or, they may string a big piece of macaroni followed by a small piece, alternating sizes.

Some children may decide to use both the macaroni and the beads. They may use a macaroni/bead/macaroni/bead pattern to

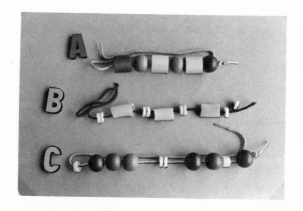

Some patterns children can make.

make a necklace. Or, they may choose a two-bead/one-macaroni pattern. Children deliberately make patterns that become very elaborate. It is not unusual, though, for them to break the pattern and begin a new one. It is not necessary for you to point this out. Should they mention it, you should accept the change and let it stand unless they want to correct it.

As in Level 1, children need to repeat these activities over and over again. Although they make different patterns, the activity is the same: they are selecting beads and/or macaroni in a predetermined order and are stringing them on the yarn.

With much repetition and practice, children can repeat a pattern from start to finish. They are less likely to break a pattern once it's begun. This consistency in patterning results from their previous stringing activities.

Level 3

In using the stringed objects as necklaces, children are getting ready for the idea of making a second necklace just like the first. Copying a pattern already made is an essential skill for children to develop.

Many children will duplicate a necklace on their own. Having made one for themselves, they ask you if you would like one just like it. Your "yes" prompts them to copy the necklace, exactly. Some children may need help in deciding to copy a pattern. You might ask them to make you a necklace "just like the one that they have." Be sure that the pattern you are asking them to copy is a simple one or the task may be too frustrating for them.

Another way you can encourage children to think about patterns is by placing some beads on a piece of yarn in a simple pattern and asking them what comes next. If you place a red bead followed by a blue bead followed by another red and then another blue, have them place the next bead on the yarn and the next and so on. Such copying and completing of patterns can be a great help for later work in school.

Possible Learning Outcomes

Number Ideas

Counting: total number on a string, number of red or blue beads, number of objects in a unit of a pattern (two red beads and one blue bead or two large beads and one small bead)

Cardinality: "oneness" and "twoness", knowing that one blue bead is followed by two red beads on the string

Ordinality: first, second, and third bead

Thinking Skills

Classifying: putting objects together by type (beads or macaroni), size, shape, or color

Planning: thinking up a design for a necklace and carrying through on that design

Patterning: creating a pattern and repeating it; copying a pattern

Measurement

Measuring length in terms of units: the length of a string in terms of beads, "This string is nine beads long."

Estimation

Estimating length by guessing how many beads will be needed to fill the string

Perceptual-motor Skills

Eye-hand coordination: stringing the beads or macaroni

Visual discrimination: selecting beads that look alike or different in size, shape, or color

Visual imagery: forming a mental picture of the necklace enables the child to select the right beads to make the necklace

ALTERNATE MATERIALS
Styrofoam packing materials, noodles, buttons
String, thin twine, or cord

2.12   Setting the Table

MATERIALS
Dishes
Flatware (knives, forks, spoons)
Paper cups and napkins
Placemats

DESCRIPTION
One of the first ways young children help their parents is by setting the table. Children often play at setting the table for themselves and a friend, either real or imaginary. You can help children do better at this by having them use a placemat, either a real one or a paper towel, for each person. This helps them focus on how many settings are needed and gives them a place to put each item in the setting.

Level 1
At first, children set a place with just a plate and a cup for each placemat. The placement of utensils if not important to them; sometimes they use them and sometimes they do not. Whether children set out a napkin often depends on whether they can see the napkins when they are setting the table. If the napkins are kept in a cabinet, the young child often forgets to put them out.

As children have more experience in using knives, forks, and spoons they will remember to set out the eating utensils. Usually their first attempts at distributing these are unsuccessful. At first not everyone will end up with a full setting or not every kind of utensil is used. Children often set out only a fork and teaspoon for each place and do not use knives and soup spoons.

Level 2
With practice, children can learn to set a complete setting. Though they put everything out on each placemat, they still have trouble knowing where things go. Their biggest problem is in deciding which side of the plate the fork goes on. This is because they have not yet mastered left and right. Even if you set one place as a model, children have a hard time copying this correct setting. In setting the place opposite the model setting, it is common for children to mirror the model by setting the fork on the right directly opposite the fork on the other side of the table, rather than placing it to the left of the plate.

Their efforts at table setting, at this level, often involve many separate trips to the kitchen. First, they get the forks and put them out. Then they go back for the spoons, then the plates, and so on.

Children often check to see if every place has exactly the same things by marching around the table and stating, as they point at the object, "fork, fork, fork, plate, plate, plate." They repeat this for every item in the setting and when they discover something missing, they fill it in.

Level 3
Gradually, children learn to reverse the placement of eating utensils for the places on the opposite side of the table. They also learn to place the napkin under the fork. At this level, children still check that each setting has the same things, but now they do it more quietly. Eventually, they will check each setting individually by thinking knife, fork, spoon, plate, napkin, and cup before going to the next setting.

Once children are comfortable doing this, they particularly enjoy demonstrating their new knowledge to the world. Even if not given the opportunity to set the table, such as in a restaurant, they willingly check each setting to see if all the items are there. They will often take the napkin off the plate and put it under the fork, and they may remark or ask about the extra spoons and glasses one often finds in a table setting in a restaurant.

At this level, children are able to get at once all the flatware needed for setting the table. Then they get the needed napkins, then the plates, and so on. They are able to do this now with fewer trips to the kitchen for two reasons. First, their counting skills have developed. Second, they are able to picture a table setting in their mind and take from the kitchen all the items they see in their mind's eye.

Children need many opportunities to practice these skills by playing at setting the table. It takes many years for most children to go from Level 1 to the end of Level 3. The typical errors children make as they gain these skills do not result from carelessness and need not always be corrected. With time and lots of chance for practice, children will learn to set a traditional table.

POSSIBLE LEARNING OUTCOMES

Ideas and Their Vocabulary

Names of items in a place setting: fork, knife, plate, cup, napkin

Place words: under (napkin under fork), on, next to, left, right

Number Ideas

One-to-one correspondence: placing one plate on each placemat

Counting: getting the correct number of forks needed to set the table before going to the table

Cardinality: "fourness", knowing that four forks, spoons, plates, cups, and napkins are needed to set the table for four people

Many-to-one correspondence: placing knife, fork, and spoon on a single placemat

Thinking Skills

Classifying: putting objects together by shape (knife, fork, spoon) or material (breakable or unbreakable)

Perceptual-motor Skills

Directionality: knowing the left and right side of the plate when setting the table

Visual imagery: forming a mental picture of a place setting enables the child to select the utensils needed

ALTERNATE MATERIALS

Besides the kitchen, the described activity can take place in a child's playroom or a dollhouse using:

Toy dishes

Paper plates, cups, and eating utensils

Pretend things such as a lid from a coffee container for a plate, an empty can for a cup, and a pencil for a knife or fork

Chapter 3   Outdoor Activities

3.1   Balancing Play

MATERIALS

Any level, stable, strip-like form such as a curb, a low wall, a log, or a crack in the sidewalk

DESCRIPTION

All children like the challenge of balancing themselves while walking on some narrow form. While doing this, their attention is focused on the balancing itself. Balancing activities are fun for children and provide several opportunities for learning.

Children often start out by balancing themselves on a crack or a line on the sidewalk. For young children, just standing with both feet on the line is a challenge. Soon they attempt to walk along the line. They carefully place one foot in front of the other while making certain that each foot is centered on the line. Each step is carefully planned. Often they extend both arms to the sides to keep themselves steady.

Their first tries at walking a crack are often unsuccessful. They step off the crack. Sometimes they actually fall down. This does not bother them and they usually go back to the starting point and begin again. They do this several times before they can keep themselves balanced as they walk along the crack.

After children can walk along a crack from one end to the other, they try turning around so that they can return to the starting point while still walking forward. Turning around requires even more balancing skill, and their first tries at this may result in their stepping off the crack. Once children are able to turn around at the end of the crack, they then try to turn around in the middle of it.

Their next challenge is to try to walk backwards while balancing on a line. Again, they need many tries before they can do this. They delight in practicing these skills over and over again.

Children repeat all these steps on different things that are too narrow for them to place their feet next to each other. They balance when they walk along a curb, a log, or any other relatively low, narrow strip.

When attempting to walk along a narrow strip which is at some distance from the ground (about 10 inches), they may want you to hold their hand. They need such support, both physical and moral. It is important for you to provide this support.

Children at all ages engage in balancing activities. However, some children find these activities very difficult. They may still be mastering walking forward while some of their same-age friends can walk backwards and turn around. Children simply need the time and freedom to progress at their own rates.

Children often invent games in which balancing plays an important role: walking a plank, follow-the-leader, or racing. Such games are often just excuses for them to do their balancing play.

Children enjoy balancing activities.

POSSIBLE LEARNING OUTCOMES

Estimation
Estimating the distance to be walked
Estimating the height of a wall a child wants to walk
along

Perceptual-motor Skills
Motor planning: thinking about where to put one's foot and
then coordinating the movements with these thoughts

ALTERNATE MATERIALS
The edge of a sandbox, a commercial balance beam, or any
piece of wood used as a path between two points

3.2   Ball Play

MATERIALS
An assortment of balls of varying sizes and weights

DESCRIPTION
Balls are one of children's favorite playthings. One special
thing about playing with a ball is that the ball can be an active
playmate. It responds when moved. A child, a wall, and a ball
can add up to many hours of active play.

For children to become more adept at ball play, they need
to understand precisely what balls can and cannot do. They can
only learn this through many hours of play. Children like to play
with balls and will often choose to spend the time needed to improve their ball-handling skills.

In order to play ball games which involve dodging, kicking,
or punching, children need to develop their catching, kicking,
and throwing skills. Each of these skills needs to be developed
separately. A complicating factor is that the best ball to help
children learn to catch is not necessarily the best ball to help
them learn to throw. Parents need to be aware of this if they
want to help their children improve specific ball-handling skills.

Rolling

Children's first experiences with balls often involve rolling balls on the ground. They test how far they roll, how fast they go, or what happens when the ball is rolled against the wall. Such play helps them to discover the many ways that balls move. Parents can help children by being their partners and rolling the ball back to them as well as encouraging them to play alone with the ball.

Throwing

It is easier for children to throw a ball than to catch it. This is because throwing a ball basically involves getting it out of one's hand. At first, children have trouble controlling how far the ball is thrown or where it goes.

Parents can help children with their throwing by having them use a light, small ball. One-handed throwing is easier to manage because children need not coordinate the movements of both hands. You should stand relatively close to the children and have them toss the ball to you. It is not important whether they use an underhand or overhand toss. The important thing is to have them succeed in getting the ball to you. As they get better at this, you can move farther away.

Children who can easily throw a light, small ball often are unable to catch such a ball. Therefore, learning how to catch should wait for another time. You may want to roll the ball back or hand it to the children before they take their next throws.

Catching

Catching a ball involves skills different from throwing. To catch, children need to estimate the speed and direction of the ball and then coordinate this estimate with the movement of their hands. They need considerable practice to become a skillful catcher.

When first learning to catch, it is best for children to use a large, light ball about the size of a soccer ball. Their first catches involve using their bodies more than their hands. Their extended arms and body form a basket into which you gently toss the ball. It is difficult for children to move to catch the ball. Therefore, the ball should come directly to them. Children need many successful experiences in catching to become confident in playing with objects that are moving toward them.

Once children can handle this kind of catching, they can be expected to catch a smaller ball in their cupped hands. Again, it is your job to toss the ball into their hands and not their job to move to the ball. Young children simply cannot coordinate those movements.

Gradually, children can be expected to move toward the ball. Stepping into the ball is easier than moving back or to the left or to the right. Children need a lot of time and practice in order to learn to catch a ball.

Children get lots of practice in throwing and catching a ball by tossing it against a wall. In this way, they can control the speed of the ball and the distance it is thrown. They like to practice on their own and can spend many hours doing this.

POSSIBLE LEARNING OUTCOMES

Ideas and Their Vocabulary
Comparative words: fast/slow, overhand/underhand
Process words: catch, roll, throw

Thinking Skills
Determining the appropriate force needed to get the ball where children want it at the speed wanted

Estimation
Estimating the distance a ball is to be thrown
Estimating the speed of a ball as it is thrown toward you

Perceptual-motor Skills
Eye-hand coordination: aiming at a target and letting go of the ball with control
Motor control: coordinating the force with which the ball is thrown and the direction in which the ball is thrown

ALTERNATE MATERIALS
Bean bags can also be used for throwing and catching activities.
NERF® balls, which are made of a soft, sponge-like material, enable children to play ball both inside and outside the house.

3.3 Collection Trips

MATERIALS
A place to walk in which various things are scattered about
A paper bag, a covered container, a basket, or big pockets

DESCRIPTION
Older children collect things. Children cherish their found treasures, whether they are baseball cards, rocks, leaves, or candy and gum wrappers. They collect, sort, and trade these items with their friends. The roots of this collection mania can be found in their activities as younger children.

Level 1
As young children walk in parks, in shopping centers, or at the beach, they spy things that interest them and pick them up and put them in their pockets. At first, they collect things for the sake of collecting. Usually, the things they collect have no relationship to each other.

Such collections are children's ways of exploring places. For example, they learn about the woods by collecting some of the things they find there. They collect leaves, acorns, and bugs. They may ask what things are called, or why they are there.

These collections are short-lived. They are important only during the actual collection process and rarely hold young children's interest once the trip is over. Parents usually have no difficulty in disposing of them.

Level 2
After many walking trips in which children casually collect things, the idea of collecting and saving certain things prompts children's explorations. They now go out to collect bugs or leaves or candy wrappers. Their walks begin with a specific purpose in mind. Often during these walks, they become interested in some object other than the one they are looking for, and they change the focus of their collection trip.

The collection has importance beyond just collecting. For one thing, children can share the experience with their friends. They check to see who has collected the most things or more different kinds of things. Such sharing expands their view of what they can collect the next time.

They spend considerable time examining their collected items. They look to see if an object is whole or broken, large or small. They also look at the whole collection to see how many objects they collected and how these objects are alike or different.

Again, they share their collections by talking about them. They want to know what things are called and where they come from.

Level 3

With older children, collection trips are usually single purpose. They go out to collect bugs, bottle caps, or leaves. They look for objects in many different places. In fact, the collection trips may last for weeks. For example, if they are interested in looking for leaves, they will collect them wherever they find them.

Typically, children organize their collection carefully. They use a special box or shelf to house it. Some children spend many hours looking at or talking about the individual objects as well as the entire collection.

Children take great pride in their collections and value them highly. Any loss or damage to a single object can be upsetting. As children become attached to their special collections, they begin to understand the value of personal property. Such an awareness can increase their sense of responsibility.

Collection trips are good vehicles for involving younger children with older children or adults. Such trips could be planned to collect recyclable materials, different kinds of leaves, or materials that can be used in making collages. Whether adult- or child-inspired, such shared experiences provide opportunities for both the children and the adults to learn about each other and the world in which they live.

POSSIBLE LEARNING OUTCOMES

Specific learning outcomes depend on the purpose and type of collection trip. In general, all collection trips contribute to the following learning outcomes.

Ideas and Their Vocabulary
    The specific ideas in this category depend on what is
    collected.

Language Development
Oral communication skills (see page 27) improve as children discuss their collections.

Thinking Skills
Classifying: putting objects together by size or shape, such as round or flat rocks, or by special characteristics, such as kinds of leaves (birch, maple, oak)

Planning: The trip — deciding what is to be collected, where to collect it, and how to bring the objects home

The collection — deciding how to organize and store an on-going collection.

ALTERNATE MATERIALS
The many possiblilties for collection trips include; leaves, shells, rocks, bottle caps, candy and gum wrappers, bugs, and acorns, nuts, and pinecones.

3.4 Identifying Cars

MATERIALS
Different real cars in traffic

DESCRIPTION
Parents often need something to keep their children occupied on long car trips. Here is an activity that has saved many a parent's sanity.

Children often describe other vehicles on the road. Comments such as "There's a car just like ours" or "Look at that red van" can be used to direct children's attention to the many ways of classifying vehicles. The purpose of this acvitity is to help children see the many ways in which cars can be alike or different.

You might ask your children to see how many different red cars they can count during a 10-mile or 10-minute trip.

Maybe they are interested in trying to identify the make of

the cars as they go by. Children often make a contest out of this by seeing who can name the make of the car first.

Here are some of the ways in which vehicles can be classified:

Two-door, four-door

Type of car: regular car (sedan), station wagon, or hatchback

American or foreign

Type of vehicle: bus, truck, recreational vehicle (RV), or van

CB antenna or no CB antenna

Stripes or no stripes

Color

Possible Learning Outcomes

Ideas and Their Vocabulary

Names of colors: blue, red, tan

Names of vehicles: bus, car, recreational vehicle (RV), truck

Thinking Skills

Classifying: identifying vehicles by color, size, or type

Classifying by negation: describing a vehicle in terms of whether it does or does not have a particular characteristic (CB or no CB, stripes or no stripes)

Alternate Materials

This activity can also be done in a large parking lot.

3.5 Painting with Water

Materials

Bucket of water

Paint brush (at least 1 inch wide)

Something to paint on (building or sidewalk)

Water is a natural resource with great appeal for children. Playing outside with water helps children to explore, experiment, and learn in a way they find particularly enjoyable. Water is a low-cost, easily accessible material that can provide children with long periods of uninterrupted play.

One particular example of outdoor water play is painting with water.

Level 1

At first, children need to explore the water and how it behaves. They might dump the water out of the bucket and watch it flow. Many try to run after the flowing water. They are particularly fascinated by the way puddles form or water runs down a crack in the sidewalk. It is not uncommon for children to spend a long time filling up the bucket, emptying it, and filling it up again.

The water in the bucket can be explored in different ways. They may drop things into the bucket and watch ripples form or use their hands to make waves and splash the water. They may also throw things in the bucket and watch some of them float and others sink. They usually try to sink those objects that do float.

Given the paint brush and the bucket of water, children explore the water with the brush. They use the brush to stir the water, often causing the water to spill over the sides of the bucket. They use the wet brush to paint the sidewalk or area around them. They make short strokes, long strokes, and spots by pressing the brush against the surface. Most likely they will try to paint themselves or any other object close by.

Level 2

At this level, long periods of time are spent painting surfaces over and over again. Some children will watch the water dry before repainting the surface. Others simply repaint the wet surface. They do, though, usually try to paint the complete surface, leaving dry no space within their reach. They repeat these activities over and over again.

Children begin to explore different kinds of brush strokes. They make a long line and a short line on the surface and watch both dry. They watch the drying process closely and talk about the different times needed for the strokes to dry.

They may paint around themselves, thereby enclosing themselves in a space. They may stand inside the space while the border dries, or they may jump over the border.

Such water play shows that when they are interested in what they are doing, children have far more patience than most adults expect them to have.

When children do this activity with another person, their language can be very extensive. They challenge each other to paint higher, wider, or longer. Not only do they practice making strokes and developing greater control over the brush, but by talking about what they are doing, they increase their language skills.

Level 3

Children at this level are more interested in what they are painting than in the painting itself. They use the water and the brush to paint a house, a hopscotch grid, or letters and numbers. They often state beforehand what they are going to paint. They particularly enjoy the challenge of trying to finish painting whatever they started to paint before the water dries. They will often touch up a section of the painting that has dried before they have finished the entire picture. On very sunny days, finishing an entire picture before any of it dries can be quite a challenge.

These paintings are planned to fill the amount of surface on which the children are able to paint. If the activity is shared, they may divide the task and assign specific parts of the picture to each painter.

A house painted with water

Such water play lends itself to forms of dramatic play. They may act out the conversation of professional painters whom they have seen at work. They will discuss the objects to be painted and make up stories about what they are doing. The evaporation of the water in parts of the picture causes them no problem. They simply repaint the part that disappeared and continue with their story.

POSSIBLE LEARNING OUTCOMES

Ideas and Their Vocabulary
Comparative words: longer/shorter, faster/slower, empty/full, wet/dry
Process words; drying, dripping

Thinking Skills
Nature of water: drips and how to control them; evaporation, the effect of sun on water; ripples caused by objects dropped into water; direction and speed of water in relation to type of surface (cement or dirt) and whether surface is level or not level
Interrelationships: it takes less time for a stroke of water painted in the sun to dry than for a stroke of water painted in the shade

Symbolic Representation
Water becomes paint and the object painted is thought of as a house or school

Measurement
Measuring length by using the child's arm span (height and width with arms held out)
Measuring area by counting the number of paint brushes of water needed to cover a certain surface

Estimation
Estimating the amount of water needed
Estimating the amount of surface needed
Estimating amount of time needed for a task (such as filling bucket) or for something to dry

Perceptual-motor Skills
Eye-hand coordination: controlling the paint brush

ALTERNATE MATERIALS

This activity can be done indoors with a smaller container of water, paint brush, and a table-top area on which to work.

3.6   Playground Play

MATERIALS

Community organized playground with such standard equipment as: merry-go-round, monkey bars, see-saws, slides, and swings

DESCRIPTION

Almost all children live in a community with a playground. This becomes the place where many children do a lot of playing. The playground, however, is not a place where young children should play unsupervised.

Also, it is important to recognize that some children are afraid to use some of this equipment. A slide is very much bigger than they are. Some children are afraid to climb up; others are afraid to slide down. Parents need to respect their children's fears. You may need to tell your children that it is all right to be afraid. You might offer to help them climb the slide. It may be just one or two steps at first. If they say no, say, "That's OK."

In saying that they do not want to play on one particular piece of equipment, they are telling you that they are concerned for their safety and often they are right. You may need to give them some safety rules to follow such as:

Use the equipment as it is supposed to be used. (Slides are for sliding down, not for climbing up. Use the ladder to climb up.)

Keep out of the path of moving swings.

A naturalistic playground, the play area of tomorrow

Traditional playgrounds are equipped with climbing equipment (monkey bars, jungle gyms, or climbers), slides, swings, merry-go-rounds, and see-saws or teeter-totters. Also, there is usually a sandbox and a wading pool. The water play (activity 3.5) and sand play (activity 3.7) described in this chapter can also take place in the playground.

Although there is a movement toward more creatively equipped playgrounds, even a traditional playground can be a place where children learn from their play. For example, climbing equipment offers many opportunitites for learning. Physical activities help children to estimate distance and require them to think before they move. While using this equipment, children often engage in dramatic play in which they act out a story. This play, no matter what the theme, helps them develop communication and problem-solving skills.

Possible Learning Outcomes

Ideas and Their Vocabulary
Action words: climbing, sliding, swinging

Comparative words: faster/slower, higher/lower, in front of/in back of
Names of equipment

Language Development
Oral communication skills (see page 27) improves as children act out stories they create as they play on the playground equipment

Thinking Skills
Creating situations to act out

Estimation
Estimating distances between parts of the climbing equipment or around the swings so that they can safely move about

Perceptual-motor Skills
Motor planning: thinking about where to put one's foot as one climbs and coordinating movements with these thoughts

ALTERNATE MATERIALS
Backyard playsets secured so that the frame is steady
Trees, tire swings

3.7 Sand Play

MATERIALS
A large sandy area
Lots of water
Assorted plastic containers and buckets
Shovels or spoons

DESCRIPTION

Sand, like water, is a resource that helps children to explore and learn in an unstructured way. Children find sand play very enjoyable, and they will spend long periods of time at such activities. Their ability to control the sand and make it do what they want it to do makes sand a material that is particularly safe, educational, and appealing to children of all ages. Sand play is an activity that can be shared with older brothers and sisters as well as with parents.

Too many extra playthings can get in the way of sand play. Four or five containers and two different-sized buckets are more than sufficient.

Level 1

At first, children simply play with the sand. They find out that sand falls through their fingers. They learn that if their hands are dry, the sand will not stick to them or is easily shaken off, but if their hands are wet, the sand sticks to them.

They work at moving the sand from one place to another. They may use their hands, feet, or backside to move the sand. They study not only the pile of sand, but also the holes or grooves they can make in the sand.

Children enjoy filling containers with sand and dumping it out. They also use the containers to fill other containers. They delight in using a large container to fill a smaller one. Unlike water play, filling a container with sand may leave a large mound on top. They usually attempt to level off the container, pushing off the extra sand. A small container may be used several times to fill a larger container. Older children may even count the number of small containers it takes to fill the larger container.

Children will repeat these activities over and over again. Through this repetition they learn all the different things that can be done with sand. They also develop a sense of the size of the individual container as well as the relative size of different containers.

Level 2

After playing with dry sand, children discover how sand changes when water is mixed with it. They learn that a container of wet sand is much heavier than a container of dry sand. They discover that wet sand sticks together better than dry sand. They use wet sand in combination with dry sand to build.

The study of wet sand occurs over long periods of time. Children make endless trips with buckets of water, filling holes with water and watching it disappear. They also use the water to make trails in the sand and enjoy watching the sand dry as the water evaporates.

They move the sand around as they did in Level 1. Now they make deep holes and fill these with water. Then they watch the sand absorb the water. If they are digging close to the water line at the beach, they may dig deep enough to discover water. They will continue to dig holes for water, but they do not understand that the water they have discovered comes from the ocean.

At this level, they begin to build with the sand. An overturned bucket of sand becomes a cake. They will try several times to make a perfect cake by adding more wet sand or packing the sand in more firmly. They will take a mound of sand and make a track around it. This track becomes a road or a moat. Often they fill this with water. If working with wet sand, they try to build a tunnel under the mound of sand. They use water to keep the sand wet and the mound together.

Their first attempts at building with sand are often unsuccessful. This usually does not bother children. They keep working at it until they are successful. They are enjoying the building rather than focusing on the structure they are making. It is the work with the sand that is important, so building something over and over again is acceptable to them.

Level 3

The structures made at this level are more complex than those at Level 2. Children usually plan structures that are more representative of the objects they are trying to make. They spend much time thinking about what they are going to make. With their greater control over the use of water, they now can use wet sand as a material in their structures. The wet sand is more easily molded and also is used for decorating. The water also plays a separate part of the construction. It becomes a moat surrounding a castle or a river under a bridge. They have no trouble seeing water in two ways, as a tool and as an entity unto itself.

Their structures demonstrate a concern for balance and

repetition of form. In building a castle they attempt to build identical columns on both sides. If they are making drip castles, they tend to repeat the pattern used on one section of the castle in another section on the other side of the castle.

Children spend very long periods of time on these activities. If they are building with a friend, the explanations of what they are doing become very detailed. Their dramatic play becomes more involved. Now the completion of the task is very important.

POSSIBLE LEARNING OUTCOMES

Ideas and Their Vocabulary
Comparative words: wet/dry, full/empty, deeper/ shallower
Descriptive words: sandy, gritty

Thinking Skills
Nature of sand: easily movable and moldable; greater packability and weight of wet sand
Patterning: creating a pattern and repeating it in the sand construction

Measurement
Measuring volume by counting the number of cups or pails of sand used to make a mountain

Estimation
Estimating amount of sand needed to build a castle
Estimating volume by guessing the number of pails or cups of water needed to fill the hole

Perceptual-motor Skills
Eye-hand coordination: pouring sand from container to container, building tunnels and moats

ALTERNATE MATERIALS
The beach is the ideal place
Sandbox and source of water

3.8   Selling Lemonade

MATERIALS
> Table, chairs or stools to sit on
> Paper
> Magic Markers or crayons
> Tape
> Lemonade in plastic pitcher
> Paper cups
> Container for money

DESCRIPTION

Selling lemonade is an activity all children like. Given some very warm days, children often suggest that they set up a lemonade stand. Because this was their idea, they will follow through on all the details and spend considerable time at this activity. Besides having a good time, selling lemonade is most children's first introduction to the business world. They can experience the viewpoint of the seller rather than the buyer.

Once young children have decided to sell lemonade, an older person should help them plan and carry out all the necessary steps. First, they must gather all the materials needed to make the lemonade and to sell it. If everything is in the house, the children may proceed with the task. To proceed without having everying on hand can be frustrating. Once the lemonade is made, they want to sell it. Having to wait because there are no paper cups in the house is difficult for them. If you need to shop for something, have them help you make a list of what is needed.

Once the lemonade is made and put in the refrigerator to cool, children are ready to make the stand. They need to get a suitable table, chairs, paper cups, and a container for the money. At this time, they probably will want to make a sign for their stand. Children enjoy using their own names on the sign. A typical sign might read "Jennifer's Lemonade Stand—5 cents a cup." Parents will need to help set a price for the lemonade. It cannot be so high that no one will buy it.

With everything now ready for the stand, it is time to set things up for this activity. You may want to talk about the best place to set up a stand where there will be people to buy the lemonade. Finding a shady place, if possible, and staying near the house are also important.

When children sell lemonade, they may either sit and wait for customers to appear, or call out "Lemonade for sale — 5 cents a cup," or whatever they think will attract customers. In any event, children are going to have to talk with the buyers. They also have to make change and deal with the fact that the lemonade is going to get warm. Solving these problems is what makes selling lemonade such an important activity.

If two children of similar ages are playing together, they may have difficulty in deciding who is to do what. Pouring, collecting the money, and keeping the stand neat are not equally desirable tasks. You may have to intervene to help them assign these tasks.

If an older child is playing with a younger child, the older child often assumes a protective, teaching role. They are usually aware that they have the greater responsibility in this activity.

After selling lemonade many times, you may want to discuss with the children the costs to you of their play activity. You may want them to share the money they collected with you so that they begin to understand it costs money to make money.

As with all other play activities, children should be expected to return all the things they used as part of their lemonade stand.

POSSIBLE LEARNING OUTCOMES

Ideas and Their Vocabulary
   Business words: buy, change, cost, sell
   Names of coins: dime, nickel, quarter

Language Development
   Oral communication skills (see page 27) improve as children talk with their customers

Number Ideas
   Value of coins: a dime is worth ten cents
   Making change

Thinking Skills
   Nature of lemonade: cooling it when first made; keeping it cool by using ice; diluting it with ice

Planning: deciding what you need, getting it, and following through on the plan for setting up the stand

Perceptual-motor Skills
Eye-hand coordination: pouring the lemonade, making a sign

ALTERNATE MATERIALS
Iced tea, juice, or punch

3.9   Street Games

MATERIALS
For Hit-the-Penny: a ball, coin, and two people
For Potsie or Hopscotch: a grid drawn on the ground as illustrated
For Hide-and-Go-Seek: any safe outdoor area with objects large enough to hide behind; three or more people

DESCRIPTION
Street games have been around forever. Their popularity comes from the fact that children need little space and equipment to play them. Such games provide opportunities for younger children to play with older children. This introduces younger children to the more involved play and social rules of the world of older children and adults.

HIT-THE-PENNY
This game is played using two squares of the sidewalk separated by a crack or a chalk diagram like the one on the next page.

Players stand at opposite ends of the boxes (points A and B). The penny is placed in the center of the line between the boxes.

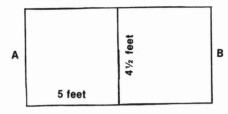

Player A throws the ball at the penny. Player B catches the ball and then takes a turn. One point is scored each time a player hits the penny. If the penny flips over, heads to tails or tails to heads, two points are scored. The first player to score eleven (11) points wins the game. If the penny, when hit, moves closer to one of the players, it is not moved back to the center.

For younger children, we suggest using a larger ball (about soccer size) and a larger coin (quarter or Susan B. Anthony dollar). Until they feel comfortable with this game, let younger children stand closer to the coin than the older children or adults do. You may want to eliminate keeping score and focus mainly on hitting the coin. As children get better at the game, keeping score maybe introduced. Eventually, you want to use a tennis-sized ball and a penny.

POSSIBLE LEARNING OUTCOMES

Ideas and Their Vocabulary
Place words: on, turn over

Number Ideas
Counting: keeping score

Thinking Skills
Determining the appropriate force needed to make the penny turn over

Estimation
Estimating the distance of the penny from the player

Perceptual-motor Skills
Eye-hand coordination: aiming at the penny

ALTERNATE MATERIALS
Various-sized balls and coins can be used.

POTSIE OR HOPSCOTCH

This popular sidewalk game is called potsie (also spelled pottsie or pottsy) or hopscotch in various parts of the country. Though there may be local rules and versions of a potsie court, the ones presented here show you typical ways young children play this game.

The potsie grid or court is drawn with chalk on the sidewalk. The potsie, usually a flat stone or key chain, is the object thrown into the boxes. This is the simplest version of a potsie court:

Some other grids are:

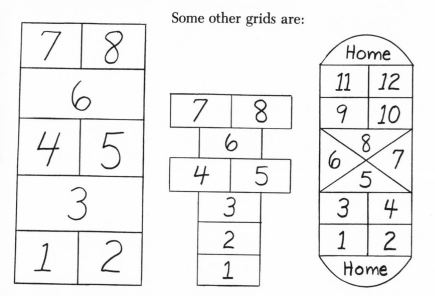

Here is a simple version of the game:

Play begins by standing outside the grid at the edge of the 1-2 boxes. The player tosses the potsie into the 1 box and then hops on one foot into the 2 and 3 boxes and lands on both feet with one foot in the 4 box and one in the 5 box. The player then hops on one foot into the 6 box and then lands on both feet with one foot in the 7 box and one in the 8 box. Now it is time to turn around and go back. The player turns around by jumping into the air and twisting around so that the opposite feet are now in the 7 and 8 boxes. Using the same hopping pattern to return, the player ends up on one foot in the 2 box and must bend down and pick up the potsie. The player then hops out of the grid and begins again by tossing the potsie in the 2 box and hopping through the grid, beginning at 1, skipping box 2, and landing in 3, 4-5, 6, and 7-8, as before. On completing the pattern in one direction, a player reverses direction, tossing the potsie into box 8 from the edge of the 7-8 boxes.

Players continue until "out," which happens when the potsie does not land in the right box, or when they touch a line when hopping through the grid, or fall down, or hop into the potsie box, or fail to pick up the potsie at the right time. On a player's next turn after going out, the player starts with the box last attempted. The first player to complete the potsie grid in both directions wins the game.

As with other streeet games, older and younger children play potsie together. With young children, you might let them walk rather than hop through the grid. It also may be necessary to have someone toss the potsie for them to the higher numbered boxes. Older children seem more than willing to bend the rules for younger children but never for children of the same age.

POSSIBLE LEARNING OUTCOMES

Ideas and Their Vocabulary
Number names: one, two
Place words: in the box, on the line, out of the box

Number Ideas
Number sequence: learning the names of numbers in the right sequence, that is, one, two, three up to eight and also from eight to one

Thinking Skills
Determining the appropriate force needed to throw the potsie into the right box

Estimation
Estimating the distance of a box from the base line

Perceptual-motor Skills
Eye-hand coordination: aiming the potsie
"Learning to read": matching number symbols with their name when spoken; for example, matching the "1" written in the box with the word one

Motor planning: thinking about where to put one's foot
and coordinating movements with these thoughts

ALTERNATE MATERIALS
Any variation on the above grids

HIDE-AND-GO-SEEK

Hide-and-Go-Seek is basically a game of tag. One player is
IT. IT covers ITs eyes while leaning against a wall or a tree and
counting to 100 by 5's. While IT is counting, the other players
run and hide. When IT reaches 100, IT shouts, "Ready or not,
here I come" and goes and seeks the others.

When IT finds someone, IT races back to home base and
shouts, "I spy Michelle by the blue car." Michelle is then caught
and has to stand by home base. If Michelle has raced back and
tagged home base before IT, then she would be free. The game
continues until IT has caught every player not home free.

While trying to catch the other players, IT must be careful
that no free player races to home base to free the captured
players by tagging the base and shouting: "Home free all." When
that happens, the game begins again with the same IT.

POSSIBLE LEARNING OUTCOMES

Number Ideas
Number sequence: learning the number names in the
five-times table by counting to 100 by 5's

Thinking Skills
Determining the appropriate speed needed to race back
to home base before IT can tag a player

Estimation
Estimating the distance between where one is hiding and
home base

Perceptual-motor Skills
Directionality: looking left and right to decide if it is safe
to run; changing direction while running away from IT

Part III   Games and Toys

Chapter 4   Card Games

CARD GAMES ARE A SOURCE of great enjoyment for children.
This activity involves them with other people and helps them
learn many things. However, if card games are to be considered
play, they must be fun.

When children play card games, they often need help shuffling the cards, dealing them out, and holding them. Holding a
set of cards in their hands, fanned out so all the cards can be seen
at once, may be difficult for children. Young children may need
to lay out the cards in their hands or hold the cards in a pack and
look at them one at a time. Another way of helping them is to use
a large spring clip or clothespin to help them hold the fanned-out
cards. Other players in a card game may have to let young
players take a longer time to play their hands as they look for the
cards they want to play.

When children are introduced to a card game, they often do
not understand or remember the rules. One way to help them

Children may have dif-
ficulty holding a fanned-
out hand.

learn the rules is to play an open game with all cards visible to all players. Another possibility is for an adult to play with a young child for the first hand or two. When children play card games, it is better for them to play out their own hands and make mistakes than it is for an adult to make their decisions for them. Although children may need help or need to be allowed to replay a card, let them make their own decisions.

Children may seem to change the rules in the middle of the game. This often happens when they do not fully understand a particular rule. They are eager to play the game and may become careless. Sometimes they change the rules by doing what comes naturally; for example, taking a peek at a card that is face down just because the child wants to know what it is. How strictly the rules are to be followed depends on the situation. For example, a winning hand should have the required cards in it and not be incomplete. If four jacks are needed and only three are shown, then you might ask where the fourth one is. On the other hand, if a child peeks at a card, you might ask if you could peek, too. Children need to follow the rules of the game, and should be gently reminded of them when they do not.

Card games are one of children's first exposures to competitive rather than cooperative play. The purpose of most games is to go out first or gain all the cards. Trying to win can present problems. Children do not like to lose and may react to losing with tears. One of the values of playing cards is that it gives them experience in losing. But it is very difficult to be a graceful loser if one never wins. Parents can decide if they want to let their chidren win a game. You must decide how often you will continue to play even though you could go out or discard a card you need because you intend to let your children win. However, if you do let your children win, let them enjoy their wins; don't tell them you could have won, if you wanted to.

One of the nice things about playing cards is that luck plays an important role. The random order of the cards is the major factor in determining who wins. Even in those games that require considerable skill, a poor hand can cause a very good player to lose. Thus, a less skilled player can often defeat a more highly skilled player. This makes playing cards a good activity for young children to do with older children or adults.

There are many different decks of cards that children can

Four of hearts, diamonds, clubs, and spades

use. Parents can buy a special deck for Animal Rummy or Go Fish, but such purchases are not necessary. All the card games discussed in this chapter can be played with a standard deck of cards. The standard deck consists of 52 cards, and a joker or two. The 52 cards can be separated into two groups, 40 number cards and 12 picture cards. The number cards are ace (one) through ten, and the picture cards are the jack, queen and king. Each card is in one of the four suits: hearts, diamonds, spades and clubs. Hearts and diamonds are red; spades and clubs are black.

Children learn many things when playing cards. First, the games are usually played in one place, and children need to stay there during the game. They need to watch which cards are played and to listen to what the other players say. Such skills will help them adjust to any situation in which they need to stay in one place while looking and listening to what other people say. Second, card games require children to follow rules or directions. They need to adjust their actions to what others do but must do so according to the rules. While following the rules, good card players learn to think ahead and plan their strategies.

In addition to the general skills that children gain from playing cards, there is some specific learning that most card games help children develop. These skills and concepts are solidified as children practice any one card game and then learn and practice other games.

DEVELOPING LANGUAGE SKILLS THROUGH CARD GAMES

Card games enhance children's communication skills. As children play cards, they often ask someone for a card. Such play helps them learn the appropriate names for the cards, as well as names of the suits and the colors of the cards. In asking for a card, they learn to ask specific questions, such as "May I have a seven?" or "Do you have a seven of hearts?" Questioning helps them learn to express in words what it is that they want.

Card games also help children develop their listening skills, particularly when there are more than two players. Children have to listen to the answers to their own questions. They must also pay attention to the questions someone else asks as well as to the answers to those questions. In addition, they must remember these answers, if only not to ask the same question again.

In order to ask and answer questions, children need to develop the vocabulary of cards. Particularly, they learn the vocabulary of plurals, that is, the name of more than one of a particular kind of card. The new words, the children's increased ability to express themselves orally, and their improved listening skills contribute to their developing language skills.

DEVELOPING MATHEMATICAL SKILLS THROUGH CARD GAMES

Cards and card games are particularly valuable as a source of mathematical learning. Thirty-six cards in the deck have numbers on them. For example, a two shows both the symbol for that number (2) and that number of objects, such as two hearts. As children handle cards, they gain a knowledge of numbers and the symbols used to write those numbers.

Many card games require that each player be dealt a certain number of cards. Other games require players to have four of a kind to "meld" or play their hands. Both of these requirements help children learn to count. Still other games call for a run of cards, for example, a three, four, and five of hearts. A run of cards helps children learn the correct sequence of numbers from lowest to highest.

Children also must be concerned with who goes first, second, third, and so on. Such number ideas, called ordinal numbers, are a part of every card game played by more than one person.

A three-card run in diamonds and a four-card run in clubs

All these skills, as well as skills gained from particular card games, are directly related to learning mathematics in school.

DEVELOPING THINKING SKILLS THROUGH CARD GAMES

Card games enable children to develop their thinking skills. At the most basic level, they group cards. That is, they put them together by color, suit, number, or particular picture (kings, queens, jacks). Such activities use classification skills. As card games become more involved, children must decide whether the color, suit, or number of the card is significant to their play. Such considerations make them think of two things at once; this is higher level reasoning.

When playing cards, players must decide what card is needed and how to get it. A player who needs a jack of hearts may play a jack of diamonds to make the other players think that jacks are unimportant. If two nines have already been played, it would be foolish to continue to collect nines, when three are needed. Children must organize their cards, take in information about the other cards played, and make a guess as to what cards are still available. Then they must decide on their winning strategy. Such decision making is the foundation of thinking skills.

The more children play cards, the more they have to think, plan ahead, and learn to adjust their plans because of new information. Card games can make children better problem solvers as they develop their thinking skills.

DEVELOPING PERCEPTUAL-MOTOR SKILLS
THROUGH CARD PLAYING

Card games provide children with experiences through which they can develop perceptual-motor skills. One of these skills, eye-hand coordination, is necessary for learning to write and for copying images.

Children develop these skills by handling cards, shuffling them, dealing them out, and adding a new card to a hand. A game such as Slap Jack, in which the first player to slap a card wins that particular turn, also helps in this development.

The ability to discriminate visually by color, shape, or number is also developed through card games. This ability is needed so that children can distinguish between different numbers, such as "42" and "24," and different words, such as "saw" and "was". Many card games require children to pick out the correct card or match one card with another after only a quick look.

Visual memory is the ability to keep a picture in one's mind of something seen before. This skill is particularly important in learning to read new words and to spell. Many card games require children not only to remember what cards have been played but also where and by whom they have been played.

Finally, card games help develop the skill of directionality. This skill is needed for children to follow a left-to-right sequence in reading, as well as in following directions in doing mathematics. As children follow the order of play in a card game, usually clockwise, and deal out cards, they have a chance to develop their sense of directionality.

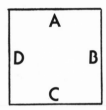

Card games are usually played clockwise: player A first, followed by players B, C, and D, in order.

The learning opportunities just discussed are common to most card games. The following sections describe several traditional and popular card games that children and adults have played throughout the years. The first four games (Slap Jack, Snap, Pisha Paysha, and War) require players to decide about each card as they see it. They do not have to remember what cards have been played. The fifth game, Concentration, requires players to remember which cards have been played and where they are located on the table. The last five games (Go Fish, Joker, Crazy Eights, I Doubt It, and Rummy) are hand-held games. They require players to look at several cards at a time and make decisions about them. Listed after each game are some particular learning outcomes for that game.

Remember, card games should be fun to play. The learning is incidental to the games. But, with practice, children can become good card players who are having a good time while developing many important skills and attitudes.

4.1 Slap Jack

DIRECTIONS

This is a game for two to four players. Deal all the cards, one at a time, to the players. Players place their stacks of cards, face down, in front of them. The game begins when the first player, A, places the first card from Player A's stack face up in the middle of the table. Play continues as each player, in turn, places a card face up on the stack in the middle of the table.

When a jack is played, the first player to slap the jack wins the entire stack of cards under it. These cards are placed face down beneath the rest of that player's cards. If several players claim to have slapped the jack first, whoever's hand is on the bottom is the winner. If two small hands are on the bottom, each covering part of the jack, continue playing without a winner for that round. A player with no cards left may continue in the game and win some cards by slapping a jack. Play continues until one player wins all the cards.

VARIATIONS

Slap the picture cards: any picture card can be the target card.

Slap a ten: any number card, say a ten, can be the target.

The time of the game can be set at, say, ten minutes. At the end of the time, the player with the most cards wins.

POSSIBLE LEARNING OUTCOMES

Perceptual-motor skills

Eye hand coordination: moving one's hand to slap the jack when it comes up. The competition of the game encourages quick motor responses

Visual discrimination: the ability to distinguish a jack (or any other specific card or cards) from all the others

4.2 Snap

DIRECTIONS

This is a game for two to four players. Deal all the cards, one at a time, to each player. Players place their stacks of cards in front of them, face down. All players take their top card from their piles and, at the same time, place it face up on the table in front of them. When two cards of the same value are turned up, the first player to say "Snap" wins all the cards that are face up. The cards won are placed face down at the bottom of the winning player's stack. Play continues until one person wins all the cards.

"Snap" is called now!

POSSIBLE LEARNING OUTCOMES

Number Ideas
Idea of equality and numeral recognition: deciding when two cards have the same value or symbol, regardless of color of suit

Perceptual-motor Skills
Visual discrimination: recognizing by sight when two cards have the same value
Quick response: encouraged by the competitiveness of the game

4.3   Pisha Paysha

DIRECTIONS

This is a game for two players. Deal each player 26 cards that are kept face down.

Both players turn cards face up at the same time, making stacks of face-up cards beside their stacks of face-down cards. When two cards of the same *suit* are turned face up, the player with the card of greater value wins all the cards facing up and places them face down at the bottom of the winning player's face-down stack.

Player A wins all the cards in both face-up stacks.

In this game, aces have the highest value, followed by kings, queens, jacks, tens, nines, and so on to twos. When there are no more cards left in a player's face-down stack, the cards in the face-up stack are turned face down and used. Play continues until one player wins all the cards.

POSSIBLE LEARNING OUTCOMES

Number Ideas

Greater than and less than: comparing two numbers and deciding which one has the greater value

Perceptual-motor Skills
Visual discrimination: looking at the cards turned face up and deciding that they are of the same suit

4.4   War

DIRECTIONS
This is a game for two players. Deal each player 26 cards that are kept face down. Both players turn their top card up. The player with the card of greater value wins the pair. In this game, aces have the highest value, followed by kings, queens, jacks, tens, nines, and so on to twos.

If both players each turn up a card of equal value, then there is a "war." Each player then deals three cards face down and turns up a fourth card. The player whose fourth card has the greater value wins the "war." If there is a tie, another "war" occurs.

When the players use all the cards in their face-down stacks, they then use the cards they have won. Play continues until one player wins all the cards.

VARIATION
Eliminate the picture cards with very young children.

Player B wins.

Possible Learning Outcomes

Number Ideas
Greater than and less than: comparing two numbers and
deciding which one has the greater value
Counting the number of cards needed to decide a "war"

4.5 Concentration

DIRECTIONS
This is a game for two to four players. Place all the cards one
at a time, face down on the table. They can be arranged in rows,
but this is not required.
The first player, player A, turns up two cards, one at a
time. If the second card matches the first in value, say both are
tens, that pair is won by the player. This player continues to play
until an unmatched pair is turned face up. These cards are then
turned face down and put back in their original place. Player B
now tries to find two cards that match. Then player C and so on.
Play continues until all pairs of cards are removed from the table.
The player with the greatest number of pairs wins.

Player B has turned
over a four and tries to
remember, "Where is
the four player A
turned over?"

VARIATIONS

Use only six to ten pairs of cards, of the same color, instead of the entire deck.

Concentration can be played by one person.

POSSIBLE LEARNING OUTCOMES

Number Ideas

Idea of equality and numeral recognition: deciding when two cards have the same value or symbol, regardless of color or suit

Idea of position in space: locating a particular card in a particular place

Thinking Skills

Planning: developing a method for remembering where a particular card is located

Perceptual-motor Skills

Visual discrimination: recognizing by sight when two cards have the same value

Visual memory: maintaining a picture in one's head of where particular cards are on the table

4.6 Go Fish

DIRECTIONS

This is a game for two to four players. Deal each player five cards. Place the rest of the deck, face down, in the middle of the playing area. Players are to hold their cards so that no other player can see them.

First, all players find all the pairs of cards in their hands which have the same value (color and suit do not matter). Each pair is placed face down in front of the player in a way that will make them easy to count at the end of the game.

Player A begins the game by asking any of the other players for a card which will match one in Player A's hand to make a

Player A has stacked the pairs won so all players can see player A has six.

pair. If player A has one jack, any player, say player C, may be asked, "Player C, do you have a jack?" If player C has a jack, it must be given to player A, who shows the pair, puts it down, and takes another turn. If player C does not have a jack, player C says, "Go Fish." Player A then takes the top card off the face-down deck in the middle of the table. If player A picked a jack, player A says, "I fished a jack," shows the card, makes a pair, and takes another turn. If a jack was not fished, it is player B's turn.

Play continues until all pairs of cards have been matched. If, during the game, a player runs out of cards, that player "fishes" the top card off the deck in the middle of the table and asks for that card. The winner is the player with the greatest number of pairs.

VARIATIONS

Instead of making pairs of cards, players must make sets of fours and ask another player for all the "sevens" or "nines" in that player's hand.

Young children can hold up the card they want and ask, "Do you have any of these?" You then can give them the correct name of the value of the card.

POSSIBLE LEARNING OUTCOMES

Language Development

Using the question form of a sentence: "Do you have a seven?"

Plurals: in the variation in which a player needs sets of four, a player asks for "sixes" or "eights"

Number Ideas
> Idea of equality and numeral recognition: deciding when two cards have the same value or symbol, regardless of color or suit
>
> Cardinality: "fourness," knowing when you have all *four* sixes or any other card
>
> Greater than and less than: comparing the number of pairs of cards that each player has and deciding who has the greatest number

Thinking Skills
> Planning: developing a plan for remembering who asked whom for what card and did not get it

Perceptual-motor Skills
> Visual discrimination: matching cards to make pairs

4.7 Joker or Old Maid*

DIRECTIONS

This is a game for two to four players., Use a deck of 52 cards and the joker. Deal all the cards, one at a time, to the players. The players make pairs of cards of the same value and place them face down on the table in front of each of them.

Player B picks one card from player A's hand without seeing the cards in player A's hand. If the card picked matches one in player B's hand, the pair is put down so that everyone can see it and then is turned over and put with the rest of player B's pairs. If it does not match any card in player B's hand, it is added to that hand. Now player C picks one card from player B, and so on.

The goal of the game is to get rid of all the cards in one's

---

*Note: This basic game has been called Old Maid. Three queens are removed from the deck at the start of the game, and the person who ends up with the odd queen is an "Old Maid." Because Old Maid is a sexist term, since it makes a negative statement about unmarried women, parents are encouraged to play the Joker version of this game.

hand by making pairs. The player who ends up with the joker is the "joker" and loses the game.

VARIATIONS

Each player gets seven cards. The remaining cards are left in a stack in the middle of the table. Whenever a player makes a pair when taking a card from another player's hand, the pair-making player takes a card from the top of this stack.

The cards in a pair must be of the same color.

POSSIBLE LEARNING OUTCOMES

Number Ideas

Idea of equality and numeral recognition: deciding when two cards have the same value or symbol regardless of color or suit

Thinking Skills

Planning: developing a method for remembering who has the joker

Perceptual-motor Skills

Visual discrimination: matching cards to make pairs by looking at them.

4.8 Crazy Eights

DIRECTIONS

This is a game for two to five players. Deal eight cards to each player. Place the rest of the deck, face down, in the middle of the playing area. Turn the top card of this stack face up beside the stack of face-down cards.

Players must match the card turned face up. Player A must match the card turned up with a card of the same value *or* the same suit. If a jack of clubs is turned up, it can be matched with any jack or any club. Player A must place the matching card, face up, on top of the jack of clubs. Player B then must match the card player A played with a card of the same value or the same suit. If a player cannot match a card played, then cards must be drawn from the face-down stack, one at a time, until a match can be made.

Eights are "wild," which means that they match any face-up card. A player who plays an eight tells the next player what suit must be played. Play continues until one player has no cards left to play. That player wins.

Either the jack of hearts or seven of clubs may be played, as well as any eight.

VARIATIONS

Any card can be the wild card. The dealer can select the wild card by calling "Crazy Nines."

POSSIBLE LEARNING OUTCOMES

Thinking Skills
Planning: developing a strategy for deciding what suit should be picked when playing an eight
Considering two ideas at once, such as card number and suit, as players look at their hands to find a card to play

Perceptual-motor Skills
Visual discrimination: looking at the card to be matched and then looking at the cards in one's hand to select a card that matches

4.9   I Doubt It

DIRECTIONS

This is a game for two to five players. Deal all the cards in the deck. Players look at their cards. Player A puts an ace face down on the table and says "one". Player B puts a two face down on top of the ace and says "two". The other players continue the game by placing a card face down and saying the next number.

If a player does not have the required card in the sequence, then a bluff is needed. The player places *any* card face down and says the correct number in the sequence. At any time during the game, a player may challenge another player. For example, if player D suspects that player B did not put down a four when saying "four", player D says, "I doubt it." Player B must turn over the card just played and show whether or not it is a four. If it is a four, the challenge is lost, and all the cards on the table must be put in player D's hand. If the card is not a four, the challenge is won, and player B must pick up all the cards. Play continues until one player has no cards. That player wins.

VARIATIONS

Eliminate the jacks, queens, and kings.

POSSIBLE LEARNING OUTCOMES

Number Ideas
Ordinality: sequencing of numbers one through ten

Thinking Skills
Decision making: deciding when to "doubt it" based on the cards played and those that are in one's hand

4.10   Rummy

DIRECTIONS

This is a game for two to four players. Deal one card at a time to each player until everyone has seven cards. Place the rest of the deck, face down, in the middle of the playing area. The goal of this game is to be the first player to have a hand with one set of three cards and one set of four cards. This is called a "rummy." A set is made with three or four cards of the same value or with a run of three or four cards (ace, two, three, or nine, ten, jack, queen) of the same suit.

Player A begins by taking the top card from the deck in the middle of the table. Player A can either discard the card picked or keep it to use as part of a set of cards. If player A keeps the card, another card from player A's hand must be discarded face up beside the face-down pile.

Player B can either take the discarded card or take the top card from the deck in the middle of the table. In either case, player B must discard a card on top of the previous discard, completely covering it. Then it is player C's turn and so on. If the face-down pile is used up, the discard pile is turned over and play continues.

Play continues until one player has a rummy. That player wins.

VARIATIONS

There are many variations of rummy, including Gin Rummy and Ten-card Rummy. Check a standard book of card games for the rules.

POSSIBLE LEARNING OUTCOMES

Number Ideas

Counting: counting the number of cards dealt; counting

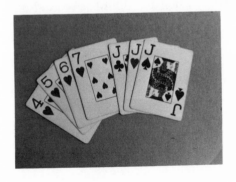

A winning Rummy hand with a run and three of a kind. Two runs or two sets, one of three of a kind and one of four of a kind, could also win.

the number of cards in a set or counting the number of tens, or any other card, already played

Ordinality: sequencing of numbers, making a run of cards

Thinking Skills

Decision making: deciding which set of cards to try for and modifying this plan based on which cards have been played or what other players seem to be collecting; deciding whether to select a certainty, the face-up card on the discard pile, or an unknown, the face-up card on top of the deck in the middle of the playing area.

Chapter 5   Rhyming and Chanting Games

CHILDREN DELIGHT IN PLAYING WITH WORDS and sounds. They make up nonsense words and laugh at the silly way they sound. They repeat their favorite rhymes and jingles over and over again as they sit in the car, play at the playground, and eat at the dinner table.

Children will chant their rhymes whether they are alone, with other children, or with adults. When two or more children chant rhymes together, this kind of play with words can last for a long time simply because chanting is so much fun. In chanting, children can imitate sounds and words they have heard as well as create new sounds and words. This satisfies a basic need for repetition and practice.

The rhythm, repetition, and imagery of children's rhyming activities enhance children's learning. In general, they help to increase children's skills in listening and following directions, in sharpening memory skills, and in concentrating. At the same time, children are channeling their excess energy in a constructive way.

All rhyming and chanting games and activities require children to be active listeners. In order to enjoy them, children must be able to remember the words and patterns and to share them. Whether the rhymes are familiar ones or a child's made-up ones, they mean something to children. Through repetition, they are beginning to solidify some important language and mathematical learning.

DEVELOPING LANGUAGE SKILLS THROUGH RHYMES

Before children can read printed words, they need many experiences hearing and speaking those words. Rhymes and chants are one way for children to have such experiences. Through rhyming, children are learning that words and language have patterns. Reciting longer rhymes requires remembering the words and the rhythms of the rhymes. It also introduces them to sequencing as they repeat words in a particular order. Patterning, sequencing, and remembering are skills basic to understanding what is read.

As children create a variety of rhythmic patterns, they need to make their own sounds and repeat or extend the sounds of other people. This increases their ability to discriminate among sounds as well as to pronounce sounds accurately. Children also capitalize on the playful quality of their voices and their growing facility with language by refining and sorting out sounds through rhymes. What they are actually doing is playing with their voices as they explore such sophisticated areas as pitch, volume, tone, and rhythm.

Children delight in using their voices to rhyme sounds. The repetition and invention of rhymes increase their understanding of our language and helps improve their oral communication skills. Whether chanting with friends or reciting a rhyme for an adult, children are using language to share ideas and feelings with others.

DEVELOPING MATHEMATICAL SKILLS THROUGH RHYMES

As in language development, children need many experiences hearing and speaking number names before they can use number symbols. Experiences with rhymes and chants help children get ready for learning the language of numbers, the skill of counting, and basic mathematical concepts.

As children use rhymes, they become familiar with the special language of mathematics. Repeating familiar and favorite rhymes gives them practice in using names of numbers in a particular order. This repetition helps them associate the sound of a number's name with the number's printed symbol.

Ryhmes also capitalize on children's fascination with rote counting. In this way, children are laying their own foundation for understanding the order of numbers and for the ability to count by two's and five's. Through repetition, children hear patterns and sequences that they will use later on.

Finally, rhymes and chants provide a way for children to

use and clarify number concepts. When children hear and use such conepts as *one more than, one half of,* and *twice as much* in their rhyming play, these ideas become familiar to them. It is easier to learn these ideas if they are already a part of their listening and speaking vocabulary.

Children have their own internal rhythm. One important way they express it is through rhymes and chants. Their fascination with repetition and rhythm helps them use chants and rhymes to learn in an easy way.

Children also use rhymes and chants for their own pleasure. They have always been a part of jump-rope games, bouncing-ball games, and chanting and clapping games and will probably remain so for future generations.

Rhymes and chants have been popular at all times throughout the world. Most chants have been passed from generation to generation through the oral tradition. Until recently, only a few of them had been written down. Because of this, the words and phrases of many chants differ somewhat from neighborhood to neighborhood and from one region to another.

Here are some traditional rhymes that appeal to children. In general, all rhymes help children to see word patterns and number patterns as well as to repeat things in sequence. They also require children to use their recall and memory skills as well as to increase their ability to distinguish among different sounds. Each rhyme, however, has specific learning possibilities associated with it.

5.1   One, Two! Buckle My Shoe

One, two, buckle my shoe;
Three, four, shut the door;
Five, six, pick up sticks;
Seven, eight, close the gate;
Nine, ten, a big fat hen;
Eleven, twelve, dig and delve;
Thirteen, fourteen, maids a-courting;
Fifteen, sixteen, maids in the kitchen;
Seventeen, eighteen, maids in waiting;
Nineteen, twenty, my plate's empty.

POSSIBLE LEARNING OUTCOMES

Language Development
Rhyming words: two/shoe, four/door

Number Ideas
Rote counting: one, two, three, and so on

5.2   One for the Money

One for the money,	(Hold up one finger.)
Two for the show,	(Hold up two fingers.)
Three to make ready,	(Hold up three fingers.)
Four to go.	(Hold up four fingers.)

POSSIBLE LEARNING OUTCOMES

Ideas and Their Vocabulary
Quantitative words: one, two, three, four (shown by holding up the correct number of fingers)

Number Ideas
Rote counting: one, two, three, four in the correct order

5.3   Five Little Pumpkins

Five little pumpkins sitting on a gate.	(Hold up a fist.)
The first one said, "Oh my, it's getting late!"	(Raise pinky finger.)
The second one said, "There are witches in the air.	(Raise ring finger.)
The third one said, "Well, I don't care."	(Raise middle finger.)
The fourth one said, "Let's run and run and run."	(Raise index finger.)
The fifth one said, "I'm ready for some fun."	(Raise thumb.)

"Oooo," went the wind,
And out went the lights,
And the five little pumpkins   (Make a fist again.)
    rolled out of sight.

POSSIBLE LEARNING OUTCOMES

Language Development
    Rhyming words: gate/late, light/sight

Number Ideas
    Ordinal number names: first, second, third

5.4 This Old Man

This old man, he played one,
    He played nick-nack on my *drum*,
Nick-nack, paddy-whack, give the dog a bone,
    This old man came rolling home.

This old man, he played two . . . shoe.
This old man, he played three . . . tree.
This old man, he played four . . . door.
This old man, he played five . . . hive.
This old man, he played six . . . sticks.
This old man, he played seven up to heaven.
This old man, he played eight . . . gate.
This old man, he played nine . . . line.
This old man, he played ten . . . hen.

Instructions
    Each time a new number is recited, hold up that number of fingers.
    Also, replace *drum* in the second line with the word that follows the dots. For example, the second verse begins with:
        This old man, he played two,
          He played nick-nack on my shoe.

POSSIBLE LEARNING OUTCOMES

Language Development
Rhyming words: three/tree, ten/hen

Number Ideas
One more than: two (fingers) is one more than one
(finger)
Rote counting: one, two, three, and so on

5.5   Ten Little Indians

One little,
  Two little,
    Three little Indians,

Four little,
  Five little,
    Six little Indians,

Seven little,
  Eight little,
    Nine little Indians,

Ten little Indian boys (*or* girls).

(From fists, raise one,
  then two, then three
  fingers, and so on.)

Ten little,
  Nine little,
    Eight little Indians,

Seven little,
  Six little,
    Five little Indians,

Four little,
  Three little,
    Two little Indians,

One little Indian girl (*or* boy).

(Curl one finger back into
  the fist, as each number
  is said.)

POSSIBLE LEARNING OUTCOMES

Ideas and Their Vocabulary
Quantitative words: one, two, three
Size words: little

Number Ideas
Rote counting, one, two, three, and so on
Counting backwards: ten, nine, eight, and so on.

One more than: two (fingers) is one more than one (finger)
One less than: four (fingers) is one less than five (fingers)

5.6   Five Green-Speckled Frogs

Five green-speckled frogs,   (Hold up five fingers.)
Sitting on a speckled log,
Eating some nice delicious bugs:
        "Yum Yum."   (Pretend to be eating.)
One jumped into the pool
Where it was nice and cool;
Then there were four   (Hold up four fingers.)
    green-speckled frogs:
        "Glub Glub."

Instructions
    Repeat, changing the numbers, down to "Then there were no green-speckled frogs *(make a fist)*./ 'Glub. Glub.'"

POSSIBLE LEARNING OUTCOMES

Ideas and Their Vocabulary
    Descriptive words: delicious, speckled
    Quantitative words: five, four, three

Language Development
    Rhyming words: pool/cool, frog/log

Number Ideas
    One less than: four (frogs) is one less than five (frogs)
    Counting backwards: five, four, and so on

5.7   London Bridge Is Falling Down

London Bridge is falling down,
   falling down, falling down,
London Bridge is falling down,
My fair lady (*or* gentleman).

Build it up with iron bars,
   iron bars, iron bars,
Build it up with iron bars,
My fair lady (*or* gentleman).

London Bridge is half built-up,
   half built-up, half built-up,
London Bridge is half built-up,
My fair lady (*or* gentleman).

London Bridge is all built-up,
   all built-up, all built-up,
London Bridge is all built-up,
My fair lady (*or* gentleman).

Take the keys and lock her (him) up,
   lock her (him) up, lock her (him) up,
Take the keys and lock her (him) up,
My fair lady (*or* gentleman).

London Bridge is falling down,
   falling down, falling down,
London Bridge is falling down,
My fair lady (*or* gentleman).

POSSIBLE LEARNING OUTCOMES

Ideas and Their Vocabulary
Action words: falling down, lock up, build up
Quantitative words: half, all

Language Development
Rhythm of language: shown by the repetition of phrases

5.8   Ra-Ta-Tat-Tat!

Ra-ta-tat-tat! Who is that?
　　Only grandpa's pussy cat.
What do you want?
　　Just some milk.
Where's your money?
　　In my pocket.
Where is your pocket?
　　I forgot it.
Oh, you silly pussy cat.

POSSIBLE LEARNING OUTCOMES

Language Development
　　Rhythm of language: ra-ta-tat-tat
　　Imagery: silly pussy cat
　　Rhyming words: that/cat

5.9   Johnny Works with One Hammer

Johnny works with one hammer,
　　one hammer, one hammer;
Johnny works with one hammer,
　　then he works with two.

(Make fist with right hand and tap on knee with it; continue through verse.)

Johnny works with two hammers,
　　two hammers, two hammers;
Johnny works with two hammers,
　　then he works with three.

(Make fists with both hands and tap on knees; continue through verse.)

Johnny works with three hammers,
　　three hammers, three hammers;
Johnny works with three hammers,
　　then he works with four.

(Tap on knees; tap right foot on floor; continue through verse.)

Johnny works with four hammers, four hammers, four hammers; Johnny works with four hammers, then he works with five.	(Tap on knees; tap both feet on floor; continue through verse.)
Johnny works with five hammers, five hammers, five hammers; Johnny works with five hammers, then he goes to sleep.	(Tap on knees; tap both feet; and move head up and down; continue through verse.)

POSSIBLE LEARNING OUTCOMES

Ideas and Their Vocabulary
Quantative words: one through five; one hand is used to tap a knee when saying "one"

Language Development
Rhythm of language: shown by the repetition of phrases

Number Ideas
Rote counting: one through five

Perceptual-motor Skills
Motor planning: thinking about what to do and then coordinating the movements with those thoughts

5.10 Cheer

Two, four, six, eight,
Who do we appreciate?
One, three, five, nine,
Who do we think is mighty fine?

POSSIBLE LEARNING OUTCOMES

Number Ideas
Counting by twos
Even and odd numbers

5.11   Head, Shoulders, Knees and Toes

Head, shoulders,
  knees and toes,
    knees and toes;
Head, shoulders,
  knees and toes,
    knees and toes;
Eyes and ears and mouth and nose;
    Head, shoulders,
      knees and toes,
      knees and toes.

(Point to or touch the body part mentioned in the rhyme.)

Instructions

Each time children have completed saying the rhyme, start it again but leave out one part of the body and say "mmm" in place of the left-out word. For example, the second time through, the rhyme would go:

"Mmm, shoulders, knees and toes, knees and toes."

Continue until children are just pointing to each body part and not saying its name. As children leave out more parts of the body, and can do this easily, they are ready to say the rhyme a little faster each time.

Possible Learning Outcomes

Ideas and Their Vocabulary
Names of body parts: shoulders, knees, toes

Language Development
Rhyming words: nose/toes

Thinking Skills
Sequencing: remembering order of body parts; remembering which body parts to point to and which ones to say out loud

Perceptual-motor Skills
Coordinating movement of hands and touching body parts while naming them

5.12 Teddy Bear

Teddy Bear, Teddy Bear turn around;   (Children may
Teddy Bear, Teddy Bear touch the ground.   make up an
Teddy Bear, Teddy Bear shine your shoe   action to
Teddy Bear, Teddy Bear I love you   suit the words.)
Teddy Bear, Teddy Bear go upstairs;
Teddy Bear, Teddy Bear say your prayers.
Teddy Bear, Teddy Bear turn out the light;
Teddy Bear, Teddy Bear say good-night.

POSSIBLE LEARNING OUTCOMES

Language Development
Rhyming words: around/ground, shoe/you
Rhythm of language: repeating Teddy Bear, Teddy Bear

5.13 The Wise Old Owl

The wise old owl lived in an oak;
The more he saw, the less he spoke;
The less he spoke, the more he heard;
And that's why he's a wise old bird.

POSSIBLE LEARNING OUTCOMES

Language Development
Rhythm of language
Imagery: wise old bird
Rhyming words: oak/spoke, heard/bird

Additional Resources
Many written collections of traditional rhymes and chants are available. The following are a few of them. Check in your local library for additional titles.

Arbuthnot, M.H., & Root, S.L. *Time for poetry* (3rd ed.). Glenview, Ill.: Scott Foresman. 1968.

Burroughs, M.T. *Did you feed my cow?* Chicago: Follett Publishing Company, 1969.

Grayson, M.F. *Let's do fingerplays.* Washington, D.C.: Robert B. Luc, Inc., 1962.

Hardendorff, J.B., compiler. *Sing Song Scuppernong.* New York: Holt, Rinehart, and Winston, 1974.

Langstaff J., & Langstaff, C., compilers. *Shimmy Shimmy Coke-Ca Pop.* Garden City, N.Y.: Doubleday, 1973.

Montgomerie, N. *This little pig went to market.* New York: Franklin Watts, Inc., 1966.

Withers, C. *A rocket in my pocket.* New York: Holt, Rinehart, and Winston, 1948.

Chapter 6 Commercial Toys and Games

CHILDREN OFTEN ASK FOR A WIDE VARIETY of toys and games. With over $100 million a year being spent on television advertising for playthings, adults need help in deciding what toys and games to buy or not to buy. Because playthings can either enhance or hinder children's play, selecting children's playthings requires much thought. Therefore, choosing such play materials for children is an important task.

Following are some guidelines that can help adults select appropriate commercial toys and games for children. These guidelines can help you to choose playthings that are good for your children and to avoid the other kinds.

Guidelines for Selecting and Using Playthings

WHAT TO LOOK FOR WHEN BUYING A TOY OR GAME
Playthings should hold children's interest. At first, the way a toy looks, its color, size, or shape, may capture children's attention. However, it is important that children can maintain continued interest in the toy over a period of time. If not, rarely used toys end up sitting on a shelf. Toys and games should be challenging, yet fun. Simply because a toy or game is attractively packaged or smartly advertised does not necessarily mean that all children will find it interesting.

Playthings should be able to be used in more than one way and by children of different ages. Children like toys and games that can be used in many ways. When children can both explore and make something with a plaything, it will be used more often. For example, when children use construction toys, they get pleasure both from stacking them one on top of another or making a building from them. Such a plaything can be used in more than one way, by more than one child, and by children of different ages.

Playthings should be durable. If children find a plaything interesting, they will use it over and over again. Such toys should be made to last so that they need not be replaced. For example, toys designed for children to sit on must be strong enough to hold their weight. Outdoor toys must be able to withstand different kinds of weather and use by children of different ages.

Playthings should be safe. Before buying playthings, make sure that they do not have sharp edges or points, small parts, or objects that are propelled, such as darts or arrows. In selecting safe toys and games, it is their construction, rather than their use, that is important. You may ask yourself:

Can I twist off the doll's head, legs, or arms?

Can I pull out the eyes of the stuffed animal?

Does the label say that the paint used is nontoxic?

Are there parts so small that a child could swallow them?

A toy or game that may be safe for older children may not be safe for younger children. Therefore, proper storage and maintenance of playthings are needed to keep children safe from some toys and games.

Playthings should contribute to children's development. Children need a balanced collection of toys and games. When a plaything challenges their imaginations, it strengthens their social, physical, emotional, and intellectual development. Providing a balance of active and quiet playthings contributes to this total growth. Children should have the chance to play with both active toys—such as balls or tricycles—and quiet playthings—such as puzzles or board games.

Playthings should help children get along with other people. If a plaything can be used by two or more children, it can contribute to children's social development. Children need opportunities to share ideas, take turns at play, and enjoy the company of others. Toys and games can help them do this.

Playthings should promote problem-solving skills. When

children are actively involved with a toy or game, they should have opportunities to experiment and create new ways of doing things. A construction toy, such as LEGO® Building Sets, enables children to set their own task and go about solving it. A board game, such as BONKERS!® , gives children a chance to plan ahead and develop strategies. Both types of activities increase children's problem-solving skills.

Playthings should be appropriate for children's abilities. If a plaything is appropriate for a particular child, the child will use it more often. Playthings that require children to manipulate very small pieces can be frustrating. That is why puzzles for young children have fewer and larger pieces than do puzzles for older children. Board games, such as MONOPOLY® , that require considerable mathematical skill, while appropriate for older children, are inappropriate for young children to play with alone. Be sure, then, to select playthings that are appropriate for children's abilities rather than playthings that appeal to you as an adult.

WHAT TO AVOID WHEN BUYING TOYS AND GAMES

In addition to the factors just discussed, here are some additional areas of concern for consideration in selecting playthings.

Avoid sex-stereotyped toys. Children need the opportunity to play with all the different kinds of toys that appeal to them. Boys enjoy holding and cuddling dolls as much as girls do. Girls enjoy building with blocks as much as boys do. Children should be provided with toys that they can enjoy for their own purposes. Adults should not bias children by preselecting the kinds of toys that children are permitted to play with. It is all right to buy a doll for a boy or a set of blocks for a girl.

Avoid buying too many toys at once. Children often become confused when given many new playthings at one time. This makes it difficult for them to decide what to play with. Given too many new playthings at one time, children may not play with any of them. It is better to purchase a few toys with many uses and help children use them in a variety of ways than to buy a large number of playthings that they are likely to play with only once or twice.

Avoid playthings that do everything for children. Playthings that do everything for children at the push of a button or turn of a key usually do not stimulate their imaginations or sustain their interest for long periods of time. Children should be actively involved with their toys and games.

Think before buying playthings that you did not have as children. Ask yourself, do your children really want or need this plaything? Or, do you really want it for yourself? Is it something that is well-made, will interest them, and will be used to enrich their play? Make sure that playthings are purchased from the point of view of the child, not of the adult.

When selecting playthings, remember that it is the play itself that is contributing to children's learning, and the play materials are only one factor in the educational value of play. Many different kinds of toys and games can be bought. Most popular types of commercial playthings fall into one of the following five categories: puzzles, construction toys, matching games, board games, and electronic games. In this chapter, each of these categories is discussed separately, and possible learning outcomes for each type of plaything are presented.

6.1   Puzzles

Puzzles are manipulative toys that are made up of two or more pieces that fit into a particular space to make a picture. Manipulative toys are materials that children handle with their hands and fingers and that require more coordination than physical strength. These kinds of materials appeal to children because they can work with them alone or with a friend or older person while they also concentrate on the act of solving the task.

Puzzles are among the oldest and most popular manipulative toys. They come in a variety of shapes, sizes, and textures. They may have a few pieces or hundreds of pieces. They come with knobs and without knobs.

Puzzles help children develop new concepts and practice some basic skills. They are designed to be self-correcting. That is, children know whether or not a piece fits and when the puzzle has been completed correctly. In addition, because they come in many textures and shapes, they are very appealing to children. This variety encourages children to use different kinds of clues when putting together the pieces of their puzzles.

Puzzles are made in many different forms and for many skill levels. It is important to select a puzzle of the appropriate skill level so that it will remain challenging but not become frustrating. Young children need to work puzzles with only few pieces. They prefer rubber or wooden puzzles because the outline of the shapes is clearer and thicker. These kinds of puzzles also help them feel, as well as see, the differences in shape.

Older children can use puzzles with more pieces. They like rubber and wooden puzzles, but they are also beginning to enjoy the challenge of jigsaw puzzles which are made out of cardboard and are more difficult to put together. In general, all children use the clues of color, shape, and size to put the pieces of a puzzle together.

Because puzzles come in so many forms and at so many skill levels, the following descriptions can help you identify the level of difficulty for selecting appropriate puzzles. They are listed in order of difficulty, from easy to more complex.

Knob Puzzles. The boards consist of individual pieces in a frame. Each piece has a knob which helps children remove and replace the pieces more easily. Both the pieces and the knobs come in larger and smaller sizes. These puzzles come in many different categories such as geometric shapes, animals, or people. Children can use the puzzle pieces in the dramatic play that facilitates their language development.

Form Boards. These boards consist of individual geometric shapes that can be easily removed and replaced. There are no knobs.

Inlaid Puzzles. These puzzles are set in a frame. The pictures are usually of a simple geometric shape or of some familiar form, such as a cat or a police officer. The simplest inlaid puzzles are usually set against a plain background to make them easier to see. Each part of the figure, such as the cat's head, is one piece. More difficult inlaid puzzles may use three or four pieces to make up the cat's head.

Differences Puzzles. These puzzles are made up of several pieces that represent the same category, such as fish, birds, or children. Each piece is a whole picture of something. All pieces

A. A form board   B. A difference board

are somewhat different so that each piece fits into only one particular place. When children use this kind of puzzle, they must
attend to small details and small variations of shape and position
which determine where the piece fits.

Jigsaw Puzzles. These puzzles usually contain many more
pieces than inlaid puzzles. Because the pieces interlock, jigsaw
puzzles require greater manual dexterity to put the pieces
together than inlaid puzzles do. The assembled pieces depict a
familiar scene or event. The clues used in deciding which pieces
fit together can be very subtle. Some children are highly
motivated by jigsaw puzzles.

As children master puzzles, they do them over and over
again in many different ways. This repetition enables them to
improve their speed and make fewer mistakes as they practice using the different clues needed to put the puzzle together. Often
they find new ways of playing with a simple puzzle that they
have mastered. Children will work their puzzles outside the
frame, backwards, and even upside down. Sometimes they take
two or three puzzles, mix the pieces together, and sort them out
again. Whatever kinds of puzzles children are using, they find
their own ways of playing with them.

There are many reasons for selecting puzzles as a toy for
children. Not only are they inexpensive, multipurpose, and

long-lasting, but also they foster many of the basic skills necessary for children to learn to read and do mathematics.

POSSIBLE LEARNING OUTCOMES

Ideas and Their Vocabulary
   Names of parts in puzzles: circle, square, oval
   Names of things in particular categories: animals (cat, dog); fruits (apple, banana); people (firefighter, letter carrier)
   Place words: next to, top, bottom, inside
Thinking Skills
   Classifying: putting puzzle pieces together by size, shape, or color
   Decision making: deciding which pieces could go on the top of the puzzle and which on the bottom of it; deciding if the puzzle is complete and, if not, changing it to make it complete

Perceptual-motor Skills
   Eye-hand coordination: picking up a piece of a puzzle and putting it into a particular place
   Visual discrimination: selecting pieces by color, shape, or size that look as if they will fit into a particular space
   Visual imagery: forming a mental picture of the puzzle enables the child to complete the puzzle outside the frame

6.2   Construction Toys

Construction toys are sets of materials with which children can build various kinds of structures. Some of the more widely available construction toys that are appropriate for young children are Construct-o-straws, LEGO® Building Sets, Lincoln Logs, Loc Bloc Construction Sets, Tinker Toys, and Tuff Stuff Wonder Blocks.

Children eagerly and naturally gravitate to this kind of toy because they enjoy making something by fitting pieces together. They also become interested in planning what they are going to build. As children develop, it becomes very important to them to build something that looks like what they are trying to build. They often make several changes in their construction to make it look as close to the real thing as possible. Using construction toys is important because, while playing, children have the chance to get better at the skills they are just beginning to learn as well as to use the skills they have already mastered. Showing that they are skillful and learning to do something new make children feel confident.

Construction toys, like unit blocks, can be used in various ways and by children of various ages. Children progress through skill levels with construction toys similar to those described in the Playing with Blocks activity. (See activity 2.8 for a more detailed discussion of this pattern of development.) Construction toys require children to fit together the pieces that come in the set. This means that they need highly developed fine motor coordination in order to enjoy using them. Therefore, children need experiences in building with standard unit blocks before they can be expected to build successfully with construction toys.

Because the pieces of construction toys fit together in so many ways, children can make cars, people, and buildings. Their constructions often look more like real objects than did their early constructions with unit blocks or their first collages. (See activities 2.2 and 2.8.)

Sets of construction toys come with booklets picturing elaborate structures. However, children are not always ready to build such complex structures yet. This often frustrates them. Therefore, encourage children to make their own structures rather than having them try to reproduce the models pictured on the box or in the instruction booklet. Copying such models will only limit their thinking to what they see there. They need to create their own construction ideas.

Through their play with construction materials, children can learn many things. It gives children chances to step back and analyze their work to see if what they have made looks as they want it to look. For example, when children are building a house with LEGO® Building Sets, they may build its frame and put in some people. As they examine it, they may realize there is no chimney or that some windows are missing. They then adjust their construction and make it look more like the picture in their heads.

The ability to make these adjustments requires children to use symbolic representation by having a picture of a house in mind and then planning the construction of it. They also must use various perceptual-motor skills. They practice visual discrimination by making all the windows the same and eye-hand coordination by selecting a piece and putting it where they want it to go.

Construction toys encourage flexibility of thought by enabling children to represent different kinds of structures while using the same materials. In building a house, for instance, children can make various kinds of houses. If it is a summer play scene, they make a beachhouse; if it is a city scene, they make an apartment house. The people they choose to put in the houses, as well as their spatial layout, would be different. Such flexibility in though, the ability to think about the same thing in different ways, is an example of divergent thinking in young children. This thinking skill is important to children as they learn to become critical readers and thinkers.

As children grow older, these sets of materials can be expanded with additional pieces in various shapes, thereby allowing children to plan and build more elaborate structures and to refine their motor skills. Many of these sets are highly durable and will last a long time while continuing to fascinate children throughout their growing years.

POSSIBLE LEARNING OUTCOMES
See activity 2.8.

6.3   Matching Games

Matching games are played with boards or tiles. They include board games such as Bingo and Lotto and tile games such as dominoes. In games of this type, children are expected to cover a symbol with a marker, such as covering "5" when five is called in Lotto, or to match a domino tile with a pattern with another tile with the same pattern. All these games can be played with others or alone. In general, there are many things children can learn from playing matching games. The greatest benefits are in the area of perceptual-motor skills.

Matching games are produced by many different manufacturers. Usually there is no real difference in similar games distributed by different companies. It is better to have one game of each type rather than several different makes of the same game.

BINGO

In Bingo, children match on their own boards the letter/number combination that is called out by the game caller. Each player receives a Bingo board and markers. The boards usually look like this:

B 1-15	I 16-30	N 31-45	G 46-60	O 61-75
2	20	38	59	71
10	17	45	53	66
7	28	31	57	62
12	30	37	54	75
4	21	42	48	61

Card X

B 1-15	I 16-30	N 31-45	G 46-60	O 61-75
6	26	35	55	63
11	30	33	47	72
8	23	40	58	64
5	16	36	46	70
9	25	44	51	74

Card Y

Commercial cards are usually developed so that the numbers in column B are between 1 and 15; in column I between 16 and 30; in column N between 31 and 45; in column G between 46 and

60; and in column O between 61 and 75. Numbers are not placed in numerical order so that the first number in a column may be greater than the second number in that column. For example, on Card X, 59, the first number in column G, is greater than 53, the second number in column G. This forces players to recognize the symbol for a number called without easily relying on a counting procedure.

A caller picks a tile which has a letter and number on it. If tile N-37 is picked, the player with card X puts a marker on that spot (see the circle on card X). If tile I-30 is picked, both players put markers on their boards (see triangles on cards X and Y). Once the tiles have been called, the caller places them on a master sheet so that a winning card can be checked against it.

The first player who gets five markers in a row, in a column, or on one of the two diagonals wins, announcing the win by calling out "BINGO!"

In addition to the general outcomes already discussed, Bingo requires children to coordinate two ideas. To identify a square on a card, both the name of the column indicated by a letter and the name of a number must be stated. Though both cards X and Y have a 30 in column I, the 30's are in different positions. The position of a number in a column is irrelevant and is ignored. Finding the proper square involves locating a point in space. The ideas for the numbers one through five are developed as children announce that they need to cover only one or two more spaces in order to win.

LOTTO

In Lotto, children match a card with a picture or symbol on it with a square on their boards that has the same picture or symbol. Play continues until one player has completely filled a board. In some Lotto games, players match identical objects such as an apple to an apple; other games have children matching pictures that go together, such as a firefighter and a fire engine.

A Lotto board is divided into six or more squares. Each player's board is different. A stack of cards containing pictures or numbers is used. The caller turns cards face up one at a time. The player whose card has a square that matches the card shown gets that card and covers up the appropriate square on the board.

In Bingo and Lotto, luck is more important than skill. They are particularly good games for young children because they are fun and easy.

DOMINO-LIKE GAMES

Domino-like games involve the matching of pieces that have identical symbols on them. Traditional dominoes are pieces made with two squares placed side-by-side. The basic set is the double-6 set, which contains 28 pieces. There are also double-9 and double-12 sets. Sets of dominoes with pictures are also available.

The next player can match three or six.

In the basic domino game, players match one square of a domino with another domino, one of whose squares is an identical match. A four must be matched with a four. If a player cannot make a match, additional dominoes must be drawn from the stack until a matching domino is drawn or there are none left to draw.

Young children can play dominoes simply as a matching game with the double-6 set or with picture dominoes. Keeping score or using the sets with more pieces should be postponed until they are comfortable with using numbers.

Both dominoes and picture dominoes contribute to children's learning. Regular dominoes introduce children to the ideas of the numbers zero through six through the use of a pattern of dots. Children also develop problem-solving skills by planning a strategy for winning. This strategy requires remembering what numbers or pictures caused an opponent to draw additional pieces and deciding how to control the game by playing the right domino.

In addition to the traditional domino sets, there are also two domino-like games that involve similar matching skills. These are Tri-Ominos and Quad-Ominos. These games require children to match the number symbols on a tile with the same symbols on another tile. Because more than one symbol needs to be matched at one time, the position of the symbols on the tiles is important.

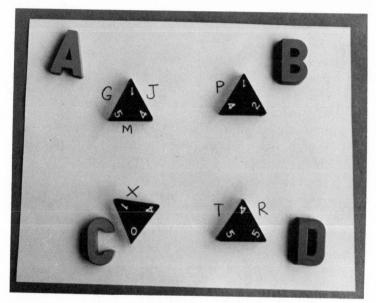

Try matching Tri-Omino A!

There are three sides of Tri-Omino A that can be matched, side G (1 and 5), side J (1 and 4), and side M (5 and 4). Side P of Tri-Omino B matches side J. There is no way that side X of Tri-Omino C can be made to match side J. At first, this bothers children because the needed numbers, 1 and 4, are present. They soon learn that the position and the specific numbers both matter.

Similarly, though both sides T and R of Tri-Omino D have a 5 and 4, only side T will match side M of Tri-Omino A. Playing Tri-Ominos and Quad-Ominos enables children to gain skill in spatial orientation, that is, seeing how the movement of a tile changes or does not change the placement of parts of the tiles.

POSSIBLE LEARNING OUTCOMES

Ideas and Their Vocabulary

Words of position: horizontal, vertical, and diagonal

Place words: in Bingo and Lotto—on top of; in domino-like games—next to

Number Ideas

Cardinality: in Bingo, knowing how many more are needed to have five squares covered in a row or column; in dominoes, knowing how many dots are on a tile

Subtraction: in Bingo, intuitively understanding that if five squares need to be covered to win and three squares are covered, then two more squares need to be covered

One-to-one correspondence: in Bingo and Lotto, matching one card to one square on a board; in domino-like games matching one side of a tile with one side of another tile

Many-to-one correspondence: A domino can be matched by two dominoes, one on each side. A Tri-Omino can be matched by three Tri-Ominos, one on each side

A Quad-Omino can be matched by four Quad-ominos, one on each side

Locating a point in space: covering a square on a Bingo board

Thinking Skills

Classifying: organizing dominoes according to the greatest number on a tile

Planning a strategy for winning in domino-like games

Decision making: deciding which tile to play based on what other tiles have been played

Coordinating two ideas: In Bingo, both a letter and a number are needed to cover a square

Perceptual-motor Skills

Eye-hand coordination: placing markers on a playing board or placing a tile next to a matching tile

Directionality: In Bingo, the ideas of horizontal, vertical, and diagonal are important; in dominoes, changing direction in placing the tiles so that they fit on the table

Visual discrimination: in Lotto, matching, by sight, a card with an apple and leaf with the same picture on a board; in a domino-like game, matching, by sight, identical patterns or symbols in order to place a tile next to another one

Auditory to visual matching: determining whether a symbol on a Bingo board, 5, matches the spoken word, *five*, which names the symbol

6.4   Board Games

Board games require players to take turns and to follow directions that are sometimes complex. Players often need to adjust their play to respond to moves made by other players. Board games can be played by children at many different ability levels. At the simplest level, there are games based totally on luck. At the most advanced level, there are board games that require complicated strategy skills. For board games to be appropriate for young children, the rules should be simple and luck should play an important role in the game.

There are three types of board games for young children. One type has a path along which players move their markers. The winner is the first player to move from the starting place to Home, or the ending place. Some games of this type are Candy Land, Chutes and Ladders, SORRY?® BONKERS!® and Parcheesi. How players move along the given path is determined by drawing a card, throwing a die or pair of dice, or twirling a spinner. Each of these devices introduces the element of chance in the game, and luck plays an important part in determining who wins. As children move along the path, they learn to count the number of spaces moved.

Younger players can play all games of this type that are based only on luck, especially Candy Land,® and Chutes and Ladders. Older players can develop their abilities to use strategies while playing games such as SORRY,® BONKERS,® and Parcheesi. The longer children play those games, the more likely it is that they will learn to consider alternate moves and select the best one to improve their chances for winning.

In the second type of board game, players move their pieces on the board according to a set of rules. Usually the goal of these games is to capture all of the other players' pieces or to be the first player all of whose pieces reach a particular place on the board. Games in this category include checkers, chinese checkers, chess, and backgammon. These games all involve the use of strategies. Only backgammon introduces the element of chance by having the players' moves determined by the throw of the dice. Therefore, it is the only one of these games in which a less skilled player can defeat a better player who is playing up to ability level. Because skill is so important in these games, young children may find them frustrating. As in playing cards, a decision must be made as to how much help a child should be given in deciding how to move, or whether a child should be permitted to win because the other player deliberately makes what seem to be mistakes.

A third type of game involves collecting things. The simplest form of such a game is Hi-Ho! Cherry-O. This game is totally based on luck, with moves determined by the players' spinning a number wheel. A more complicated collection game which young children can begin to play along with an older child or adult is MONOPOLY.® Strategies and planning ahead, as well as luck, are important to this game. Both games are appropriate for young children. Hi-Ho! Cherry-O can be played by young children independent of adults; MONOPOLY®cannot.

Board games are available at many different levels of difficulty. The games mentioned here are some of the all-time favorites. Each year many new games appear on the market. The selection of board games for young children should be based on the children's interests. Many of these games will continue to be popular with children as they grow older, for as they develop skills at playing board games, strategy becomes more important and luck becomes less so. Each game has its own set of possible learning outcomes. The following list indicates only some of the possible learning that may be gained by playing board games.

POSSIBLE LEARNING OUTCOMES

Number Ideas
> Counting: number of spaces to be moved; in Hi-Ho! Cherry-O, the number of cherries collected
> Money concepts: buying and selling in MONOPOLY®

Thinking Skills
> Planning and decision making: in BONKERS® planning a strategy for placing the instruction cards; in checkers, setting up a double jump; in backgammon, deciding where to leave a "blot"

Perceptual-motor Skills
> Directionality: order of play around the board; movement of pieces on the board
> Visual discrimination: in Candy Land, matching, by sight, the color on a card with the color of the squares on the path

6.5   Electronic Games

Most electronic games are battery-operated toys in which one or two children play a game against a computer. These toys are available in many areas of interest and provide games of skill for children of all ages. Most of them have two or more skill levels, speeds, game variations, and types of response. They can be either hand-held or played on a table-top. Some games can be played by one person against the computer; others can be played by two people against each other. Examples of some electronic games which have proven to hold children's attention and interest are Alpha-Probe; Alphie; Major-Morgan, The Electronic Organ; MERLIN™; and Simon.

In general, electronic games have many advantages. First, they require children's active involvement. Without their active participation, there can be no game. The result of such involvement helps children develop problem-solving strategies as they use memory to remember sequences and patterns in order to "beat the computer." These skills are further enhanced through the immediate feedback children receive from the computer when playing electronic games.

A second advantage of electronic games is that they can be played by either sex. Whether they are word or number games or sports or card games, they can be played by anyone at any time. Electronic games give all children the same chance to participate in those games and activities in which they are most interested. Girls who might not have considered playing football outside can play electronic football and learn about that game. This is a major breakthrough in terms of shaping new attitudes toward play by children of both sexes.

A further advantage of electronic toys is that they capitalize on and help develop children's perceptual-motor skills. These games require children to develop their eye-hand coordination and to improve their timing. Through practice, children learn how to use a quick response to get what they want from the computer.

Although there are more advantages than disadvantages to electronic games, they do have some drawbacks. The major one is cost; they are very expensive, not only initially, but with the continuing cost of replacing batteries. However, most popular electronic games can be purchased at a discount from the manufacturer's suggested retail price. It pays to shop around because the range in prices is considerable. Local consumer affairs groups often publish annual price and safety reports of toys. These are often reported through local news media in early December.

In addition to cost, children's interest in electronic games is often short-lived. Initially, these toys are most fascinating because of their bright light and sound effects. Soon, however, they wind up on a shelf. This is because, more often than not, children are not sufficiently challenged once they have mastered the specific games, and such games do not encourage interaction with other people.

Most electronic games are well-constructed, attractive, and durable. Nevertheless, parents are encouraged to weigh the cost of such games against their potential use.

POSSIBLE LEARNING OUTCOMES

Thinking Skills
Patterning: remembering the sequences and patterns in each game in order to "beat the computer"

Perceptual-motor Skills
Eye-hand coordination: moving one's hand to activate the computer and make it do what you want it to do. The timing of these games encourages quick responses
Auditory memory: the ability to hold a sound or sound pattern in mind and repeat it

Appendices

Appendix A

Glossary of Special Terms
and
Cross-referenced Chart of
Skills by Activities

Appendix A contains a chart that enables the reader to identify the activities in which children can have experiences with specific learning outcomes. The left-hand column of the chart lists the major outcomes identified from all the *Possible Learning Outcomes* found at the end of each activity. To the right of the list of learning outcomes, the squares contain the numbers of those activities, by chapter, through which children can gain experience with that idea or skill

If you are concerned with developing classification skills, look down the left-hand column until you see *Classifying.* In the squares to the right of *Classifying,* you will find the numbers of those activities in which your children can have experiences with classification skills. For *Classifying,* the activities are 2.1, 2.2, 2.7, 2.8, 2.9, 2.11, and 2.12; 3.3 and 3.4; and 6.1, 6.2, and 6.3.

All the activities in this book introduce children to ideas and their vocabulary, as well as providing opportunities for the development of oral communication skills. The degree to which children can benefit in these areas depends upon the degree of their interactions with other children and adults. The particular activities listed next to *Oral communication* are those in which a primary part of the activities involves discussions by the children of what they are doing.

Though this chart can help in the selection of play activities for young children, it should not be used too frequently. Remember, for children's activities to be play, they must be fun and voluntary.

GLOSSARY OF SPECIAL TERMS

This glossary of special terms is presented in the same order as are the categories in the cross-referenced chart. Though all these words were defined in the text as they were introduced, this glossary will enable you to recall the meanings of these special words without having to refer back to the text.

Ideas and Their Vocabulary: As children interact with the people, things, and events in their world, they need the words to describe their experiences. This category has examples of the words that children will need in order to talk about the ideas they gain from the specific activities.

Language Development: As children talk about ideas, they need to develop skills in using words so they can better communicate with others. This category details ways in which children can improve their use of language.

> *Oral communication:* The ability to talk with others and understand what they are saying.

Number Ideas: As children order their world in quantitative ways, they must deal with many number concepts. This category includes those concepts and processes in mathematics, other than measurement and estimation, that children can learn through play.

> *One-to-one correspondence:* The matching of one object (either real or symbolic) with another object. The matching may be either physical or mental.
>
> *Cardinality:* The answer to the question "how many" without, necessarily, having to count out the objects, such as knowing that there are *four* people in a family.
>
> *Ordinality:* The answer to the question "which one in numerical order," such as first, third, or last.

Thinking Skills: As children solve problems, they engage in mental processes that become more refined with experience. This category includes some of those processes that are most important to the development of reasoning.

Classifying: Putting objects together by some particular characteristic(s), such as color, size, or weight.

Seriation: Putting objects in order according to size (largest to smallest) or value (least to greatest, such as 1 before 2 before 3).

Symbolic Representation: As children need to refer to objects that are not physically present, they need the ability to mentally create those objects. This category details ways in which specific activities provide experiences in which children mentally create an object so that they can use something else to be the object they have imagined. For example, children think of a sandwich and know to use three pieces of paper to be a pretend sandwich.

Measurement: As children explore their world, they often need to describe objects with regard to their length, volume, or area. This category lists those activities in which children learn these ideas.

Estimation: Children must often make guesses about distance, volume, or area. This category lists those activities in which children have to make such guesses.

Perceptual-motor Skills: As children play, they need to coordinate the information acquired through their senses with what their brains need to tell their muscles to do. This category includes some of these specific skills.

Eye-hand coordination: Making your hand be where your eye wants it to be.

Directionality: Getting from one place to another along a definite path.

Visual discrimination: Determining by sight whether things are alike or different.

Visual imagery: Forming a mental picture of an object that is not present to enable planning as a similar object is made.

ACTIVITIES CLASSIFIED BY LEARNING OUTCOMES

Learning Outcomes	2	3	Chapters 4	5	6
Ideas and Their Vocabulary	All	All	All	All	All
Language Development					
Oral communication	All, 2.3, 2.5	All, 3.3, 3.6, 3.8	All	All	All
Rhyming words				5.1, 5.3, 5.4, 5.6, 5.8, 5.11, 5.12, 5.13	
Other	2.4, 2.9		4.6	5.7, 5.8, 5.9, 5.12, 5.13	

Learning Outcomes	2	3	Chapters 4	5	6
Number Ideas Counting	2.1, 2.8, 2.9, 2.11, 2.12	3.9	4.4, 4.10	5.1, 5.2, 5.4, 5.5, 5.9, 5.10	6.2, 6.4
One-to-one correspondence	2.1, 2.8, 2.9, 2.12				6.2, 6.3
Cardinality	2.1, 2.8, 2.11, 2.12		4.6		6.2, 6.3
Ordinality	2.11		4.9, 4.10	5.3	
Equality and inequality			4.2, 4.3, 4.4, 4.5, 4.6, 4.7		
Other	2.1, 2.8, 2.12	3.8, 3.9	4.5	5.4, 5.5, 5.6, 5.10	6.2, 6.3, 6.4

ACTIVITIES CLASSIFIED BY LEARNING OUTCOMES (CONT.)

Learning Outcomes	2	3	Chapters 4	5	6
Thinking Skills					
Nature of materials	2.4, 2.6 2.8, 2.9	3.5, 3.7, 3.8			
Classifying	2.1, 2.2, 2.7, 2.8, 2.9, 2.11, 2.12	3.3, 3.4			6.1, 6.2, 6.3
Planning	2.2, 2.4, 2.5, 2.6, 2.8, 2.10, 2.11	3.3, 3.8	4.5, 4.6, 4.7, 4.8		6.2, 6.3, 6.4
Decision making			4.9, 4.10		6.1, 6.3, 6.4
Patterning	2.8, 2.11	3.7			6.5, 6.2

Learning Outcomes	2	3	Chapters 4	5	6
Seriation	2.1, 2.7, 2.9				
Other	2.3, 2.4 2.5, 2.6, 2.9, 2.10	3.2, 3.4, 3.5, 3.6, 3.9	4.8	5.11	6.3
Symbolic Representation	2.2, 2.3, 2.5, 2.6	3.5			
Measurement	2.4, 2.6, 2.7, 2.8, 2.11	3.5, 3.7			6.2
Estimation	2.2, 2.4, 2.6, 2.8, 2.10, 2.11	3.1, 3.2, 3.5, 3.6, 3.7, 3.9			6.2

ACTIVITIES CLASSIFIED BY LEARNING OUTCOMES (CONT.)

Learning Outcomes	2	3	Chapters 4	5	6
Perceptual-motor Skills					
Eye-hand coordination	2.2, 2.7, 2.8, 2.9, 2.10, 2.11	3.2, 3.5, 3.7, 3.8, 3.9	All, 4.1		6.1, 6.2, 6.3, 6.5
Directionality	2.8, 2.10, 2.12	3.9	All		6.2, 6.3, 6.4
Visual discrimination	2.2, 2.8, 2.11		4.1, 4.2, 4.3, 4.5, 4.6, 4.7, 4.8		6.1, 6.2, 6.3, 6.4
Visual imagery	2.2, 2.3, 2.5, 2.6, 2.8, 2.11, 2.12				6.1, 6.2
Other		3.1, 3.2, 3.6, 3.9	4.2, 4.5	5.9, 5.11	6.2, 6.3, 6.5

Appendix B

Common Household Objects
and "Junk" Materials
Used as Playthings

Children often use common household objects as playthings. Plastic containers can not only be used for storage, but can also be stacked one on top of another to make a tower. Whether a particular household item is to be used as a plaything must be determined individually. The possibilities of varied uses exist with many different household items.

Using "junk" materials as playthings has several advantages. Such things are inexpensive, easily available, and provide children with limitless possibilities in their play. The varied ways children find to use them challenge their imaginations and increase the possibilities for learning.

For "junk" materials to be useful, they need to be accessible. By saving things that normally would be discarded, a collection of assorted, interesting playthings can be created. This collection can be stored in one box that is clearly identified as containing playthings.

Appendix B lists only the major household objects and "junk" materials identified in the activities described in Chapters 2 and 3. These materials are grouped into five general categories. The name of each category is followed by a brief statement. The numbers of the activities in which each of the materials is listed are indicated next to those materials.

Basic Supplies. There are some basic household supplies that greatly enhance children's play. Having these available for children's use enables them to engage in a wide variety of activities.

Beads (2.11); blunt-point needles (2.10); clay or

plasticine (2.6); felt-tip pens or crayons (3.8); glue or paste (2.2); masking or cellophane tape (3.8); paint brushes (3.5); scissors (2.2, 2.10); string, thin twine, cord, yarn, or thread (2.10, 2.11).

Collectibles. People save many things that they think may be useful in the future. Such "collectibles" can become valuable children's playthings.

Buttons (2.1, 2.2, 2.10, 2.11); coins (2.1, 2.9); sequins (2.10).

Things from the Kitchen and Pantry. A major source of children's playthings is the kitchen and pantry. Children want to play with those things they find all around them. A decision must be made as to which common household items can be used as playthings.

Dishes and eating utensils (2.4, 2.9, 2.12, 3.8); measuring cups and spoons (2.4, 2.7, 3.7); paper cups and plates (3.8); pots 'n' pans (2.4, 2.6, 2.9).

Assorted beans (2.1); M & M candies (2.1); noodles and macaroni (2.1, 2.11).

Assorted plastic containers and bottles with lids (2.4, 2.6, 2.7, 2.9, 2.12, 3.3, 3.7); buckets and cans (2.7, 3.5, 3.7).

Egg cartons (2.1); paper toweling and toilet paper rolls (2.2); waxed paper (2.6).

Recycled Materials. Before you discard seemingly useless materials, consider how children can use them in their play. The saving of odds 'n' ends similiar to the items listed will provide children with a wide variety of creative playthings.

Old clothes, shoes, bags and hats (2.3); paper scraps, waxed paper, and cardboard (2.1, 2.2, 2.6, 3.8); popsicle sticks (2.2); scraps of materials such as felt, pieces of foam, and ribbon (2.1, 2.2, 2.10); styrofoam packing materials and trays (2.10, 2.11).

Other. The list of things that children choose to play with is endless.

Assorted balls (3.2, 3.9); bean bags (3.2); shovels (3.7).

Appendix C

Manufacturers and Distributors of Toys and Games

Some of the manufacturers and distributors of commercial toys and games that are appropriate for young children are listed here. Toy manufacturers usually place their products into general categories similiar to those used in Chapter 6. Their catalogs show what puzzles, board games, construction toys, and electronic games they produce. Many manufacturers will send catalogs upon written request.

For each manufacturer listed, a name and address is given, followed by the general categories of products marketed by that company. This is accompanied by the names of some of the manufacturer's more popular products, many of which were mentioned in Chapter 6.

Manufacturers	Products
Cadaco, Inc. 310 W. Polk Chicago, IL 60607	Board games, electronic games
Childcraft Education Corp. 20 Kilmer Road Edison Township, NJ 08817	Puzzles (Zoo Puzzle, knob puzzles, jigsaw puzzles) Construction toys (Unit Building blocks, Blockbusters) Art materials (Collage Set, Caran D'Ache Modeling Set, Perma-Clay) Balls (Lunar Balls, Wonder Balls) Housekeeping (Tea Set, Aluminum Flatware, Kitchen Utensils)

Manufacturers	Products
Creative Playthings Princeton, NJ 08540	Puzzles (Busy Tryboard) Construction toys (hardwood blocks)
EDU-Cards Corporation Binney & Smith, Inc. Easton, PA 18042	Picture dominoes
Entex Industries, Inc. 303 West Artesia Blvd. Compton, CA 90220	Construction toys (Loc Blocs) Electronic games
Fisher-Price Toys 620 Girard Avenue East Aurora, NY 14052	Puzzles (assorted wood puzzles) Housekeeping (kitchen set) Electronic games (Alpha-Probe)
Gilbert Industries, Inc. Long Meadow Road P.O. Box 980 Hagerstown, MD 21740	Construction toys (Young Erector Set)
Hasbro Industries, Inc. 1027 Newport Avenue Pawtucket, RI 02861	Electronic games Mr. Potato Head
Instructo® Corporation Paoli, PA 19301	Matching-color dominoes
Kenner Products Company 912 Sycamore Street Cincinnati, OH 45202	Art materials (Play-Doh)
Knickerbocker Toy Company, Inc. 207 Pond Avenue Middlesex, NJ 08846	Construction toys (Toy Builder Sets)
LEGO Systems Inc. 555 Taylor Road Enfield, CT 06082	Construction toys (LEGO® Building Sets)
Mattel, Inc. 5150 Rosecrans Avenue Hawthorne, CA 90250	Construction Toys (Tuff Stuff Wonder Blocks) Electronic games

Manufacturers	Products
Milton Bradley, Inc.* 1500 Main Street Springfield, MA 01115	Board Games (Candy Land®) Electronic games (Simon™)

*Both products listed above are trademarks of
Milton Bradley, Inc.

Parker Brothers 50-T Dunham Road Beverly, MA 01915	Board games (MONOPOLY® , BONKERS!®, SORRY®, Winnie the Pooh®, The Uncle Wiggly Game®) Construction toys (Blockhead!®) Balls (Nerf® products) Electronic games (Merlin™)

*All names of products listed above are trademarks of
Parker Brothers.

Playskool, Inc. 4501 W. Augusta Blvd. Chicago, IL 60651	Construction toys (wood blocks, colored and natural; Lincoln Logs) Beads (Jumbo Wood Beads) Electronic games (Alphie; Major Morgan, The Electronic Organ) Puzzles (large selection of puzzles at different levels of difficulty)
Pressman Toy Corporation 745 Joyce Kilmer Avenue New Brunswick, NJ 08901	Tri-Ominos, Quad-Ominos, Pic- ture Tri-Ominos Sewing cards
Tonka Corporation 10505 Wayzata Blvd. Hopkins, MN 55343	Construction toys (Builder Play- sets)
Western Stamping Corp. 2218-T Enterprise Avenue Jackson, MI 49203	Tom Thumb cash register
Western Publishing Company, Inc. Racine, WI 53404	Bingo

Appendix D

Additional Resources

There are many sources of information on how imporatnt play is for children. Much has also been written on selecting safe toys.

The following list contains some additional resources that may be of interest to you.

Canadian Association of Toy Lending Libraries
50 Quebec Avenue
Toronto, Ontario M6P 4B4 Canada

Children's Advertising Review Unit — NAD
845 Third Avenue
New York, NY 10022

Consumer Affairs Committee
Americans for Democratic Action
Room 850, 1411 K Street, N.W.
Washington, DC 20005

> *Annual Toy Price and Safety Survey* $5.00
> *Published in December each year*

Consumer Information Center
Pueblo, CO 81009

> Two pamphlets: *Beautiful Junk*   0005F $0.40
>   *Safe Toy Tips*   641F   Free

Consumer Product Safety Commission
5400 West Bard Avenue
Besthesda, MD 20207

> Products that have met the commission's safety standards usually have "PS72-76" marked somewhere on the package.

> Hot Line Toll Free Numbers: 800-638-8326 or (for Maryland) 800-492-8363
> For information requesting its toy safety packet or reporting defective or dangerous products

Fisher-Price Toys
620 Girard Avenue
East Aurora, NY 14052

> A brief article: "Determining age appropriateness and relevance of Fisher-Price toys"

> A booklet: *Fisher-Price Toys in Brief*

Hasbro Industries, Inc.
1027 Newport Avenue
Pawtucket, RI 02861

> A booklet: *The Wonderful World of Play*

Joseph P. Kennedy Jr. Foundation
1701 K Street, N.W.
Washington, DC 20006

> A kit of twelve playguides for parents and teachers of handicapped or retarded children

> *Let's Play to Grow* $2.50

Mattel, Inc.
5150 Rosecrans Avenue
Hawthorne, CA 90250

> A pamphlet: *Toy Buying Guide for Grown-Ups*

Playskool Inc.
4501 W. Augusta Blvd.
Chicago, IL 60651

> A booklet on the right toy for the right age: *Playtools*

Toy Manufacturers of America, Inc.
200 Fifth Avenue, Room 740
New York, NY 10010

A set of four consumer information pamphlets containing information about the significance of toys and their proper purchase and use:
Choosing Toys for Children
Parents Are the First Playmates
Toys Are Teaching Tools
Playing Safely with Toys

U.S. Government Printing Office
Washington, DC 20402

Two pamphlets:
Beautiful Junk 017-092-00004-9		$1.50
Toys: Fun in the Making *017-090-00052-6*		$1.50

Two articles of particular interest:
Singer, D. "Parents as partners,"
Parents' Magazine, May, 1980.
Sutton-Smith, B. "Play isn't just kid stuff,"
Parents' Magazine, August, 1978.

859 2